Praise for

Hacks

"Explosive....[Brazile] has every right to tell her story. And don't expect her to ask anyone for permission."

—Ruben Navarrette, syndicated columnist,
Washington Post Writers Group

"With bracing honesty, enchanting self-awareness, and a wonderful storyteller's voice, Donna Brazile recounts the fascinating inside story of the 2016 campaign and what it was like being hacked. It is a deeply emotional story, but she tells it with great humor and insight."

—Walter Isaacson, #1 *New York Times*
bestselling author of *Leonardo da Vinci*

"The former DNC chair's memoir of election defeat has it all....Brazile most certainly has a story to tell....An easy and vivid read, everything one expects in a first-person campaign narrative—except for its detailed discussion of Russia's hacks, WikiLeaks, and threats to Brazile herself. On that score, the book is downright alarming."

—*The Guardian*

"Donna Brazile is one of the truly brilliant minds in the Democratic Party, and she's venting her frustration on the way she was treated, and frankly she has every right to do so....And frankly people should sit up, take notes, and change things instead of carping about it."

—Ace Smith, *Los Angeles Times*

"[Brazile] does have a story to tell that the Democrats shouldn't dismiss, if they intend to win the White House in 2020....The book is a fun read....The conjunction of Brazile's indiscreet book...suggests that talking bluntly about the Party's mistakes might not be a hindrance. A dose of [Brazile's] Dolores might even help."

—Amy Davidson Sorkin, *The New Yorker*

"[Brazile] had a front-row seat to everything that happened....That's where we are today: spies and lies; technocrats and math; fake populism and bad algorithms. How far we have gone from the noble causes for which people like Donna Brazile once signed up."

—Thomas Frank, *The Guardian*

Hacks

ALSO BY DONNA BRAZILE

Cooking with Grease: Stirring the Pots in American Politics

Hacks

The Inside Story of the
Break-ins and Breakdowns
That Put Donald Trump in
the White House

Donna Brazile

NEW YORK   BOSTON

Hachette Books
Hachette Book Group
1290 Avenue of the Americas
New York, NY 10104
hachettebooks.com
twitter.com/hachettebooks

Originally published as a hardcover and ebook in 2017 by Hachette Books, Inc.

First trade paperback edition: November 2018

Hachette Books is a division of Hachette Book Group, Inc.

The Hachette Books name and logo are trademarks of Hachette Book Group, Inc.

The publisher is not responsible for websites (or their content) that are not owned
by the publisher.

The Hachette Speakers Bureau provides a wide range of authors for speaking
events. To find out more, go to www.hachettespeakersbureau.com or call
(866) 376-6591.

Print book interior design by Timothy Shaner, NightandDayDesign.biz

LCCN: 2017947273
ISBN: 978-0-316-47850-2

Printed in the United States of America

LSC-C

10 9 8 7 6 5 4 3 2 1

In loving memory of my father, Lionel Brazile Sr.,
my beloved sister, Sheila Brazile,
my fearless uncles Nat, Floyd, and Douglas,
Harlem's finest, my aunt Lucille,
my friend and mentor, David Kaufmann,
my DNC colleague and patriot, Seth Rich,
and my beloved Pomeranian, Chip Joshua
Marvin Brazile (Booty Wipes).
I miss y'all. . . .

CONTENTS

There are some things you learn best in calm, and some in storm.

—WILLA CATHER

The Phone Call

When the name HILLARY CLINTON popped up on my phone in February 2017, I realized hers was a call I'd stopped waiting to receive. On Election Day, the tradition in politics is that candidates personally thank the people who helped most in the campaign. Win or lose, in the days that follow, the candidate extends that circle of gratitude to members of the party and the donors. Bernie Sanders called me on November 9, 2016, and Joe Biden, too. The vice president even came to our staff holiday party. But I never heard from Hillary.

I figured she might be hurting too bad to make that call. I had a tender spot for Hillary. I sympathized with everything she had gone through in the wretched election of 2016. I had been through plenty of rough campaigns in my forty years in politics, but I had never seen anything like the viciousness and turmoil of that horrible season as I fought alongside her. The only thing that was keeping me going as we faced the blazing fury of Donald Trump, when I was getting hit every day and thinking I just wanted to stop, was knowing my friend Hillary was getting the shit kicked out of her, too. *Look at what they are doing to her, how they are destroying her*, I'd think. I felt a duty to Hillary that went far beyond just being the chair of the Democratic Party.

We had met when I was still in my twenties. I was working as a consultant at the Children's Defense Fund in the 1980s, which was where I met Hillary. I was a high-minded, strong-willed young woman who, through my aptitude for politics, crawled out of poverty in Louisiana to a career in Washington, DC. Hillary was one of my idols. While I was rough and bossy, Hillary was cool and smooth, polished by the Ivy League, and comfortable in the halls of power. Also, she was fearless fighting for children's rights, and I saw in her many qualities I wanted to make stronger in myself.

I never forgot that it was Hillary in 2003 who told some of the party leaders to pay attention to a talented young Illinois state senator named Barack Obama. Without that assist from Hillary, Obama would not have been offered the keynote at the 2004 Democratic National Convention and almost certainly would not have gone on to become the first black president. Hillary's gesture back then always stayed with me. So when several decades later, I suddenly was asked to serve again as interim party chair on the eve of the Democratic Convention in July 2016, just until she won in November, I couldn't say no.

But I wanted to. I had promised myself, after I managed Al Gore's campaign in 2000, that I never would let politics break my heart again. Acting as a media surrogate and staunch supporter of the team that got the first black president elected more than healed that wound. Getting Obama reelected was joy. So when I was asked to serve as interim chair—for what would be my second stint in this thankless job—I decided I had one more fight left in me, and a noble one at that. I could help get the first woman president elected. After she won, Hillary's staff would assume control of the party. I could dance out the door to the sweet music of victory and go back to my perfect life. I never could have guessed how the months that followed would alter my life—and my country—forever.

Instead of being able to dance out the door in November, I had to stay through the end of February to perform the somber duties of the defeated: the painstaking work of filing all the financial reports with the Federal Election Commission, filing similar reports in all fifty states and the District of Columbia, shutting down offices, laying off thousands of people.

After that disastrous Election Day I didn't want to think about politics or talk about it, and I was guessing Hillary felt that way and worse: that she had blown this chance and had let her sisters down. My heart went out to her. No matter how strong our differences were in the campaign, I know she is a good woman. I heard from time to time that she was asking about me, but I never took it seriously. She had all my numbers. I knew what I wanted to say to her and it was: *I have nothing but respect for you for being so brave and classy considering everything that went on.* But in the weeks after the loss, every time I checked my phone thinking I might have missed her call, it wasn't her.

After the loss, the Democrats went into hiding, or started picking through the carnage, while the country was hungry for answers from a party that honestly didn't know what to say. We had lost to Donald Trump! How was that possible? And what did we have to do to make sure that didn't happen the next time?

It took me until the end of the year, after a holiday in Hawaii, to start getting my mojo back. We needed to remember that Hillary had won the popular vote. We did not have to hang our heads in shame. No, we had to find a way to stand this party back up if we were ever to have a chance to win again.

What inspired me was my kids, all 150 of them. I've never given birth to a child, but politics is a family affair. In a campaign, you see what the others are made of, you see people under pressure, and you see their limits tested in triumph and defeat. You get to know one another, in ways better than you do members of your real family. When I spotted young people with a real spark, that true combination of idealism and cunning essential to surviving in politics, I found work for them. Those were my kids, ages twenty-two to forty-five, scattered all around the country. I wanted to rebuild the party to give them a chance to lead.

Back in December when I thought about what the party could do, what I could do, I remembered how Terry McAuliffe took over as Democratic National Committee chair after our loss in 2000 and how Howard Dean stepped up after the defeat of then U.S. senator John Kerry in 2004. They reached out to the voters to understand what the party had gotten wrong about the mood of the country. They wanted to let the grassroots decide the future direction of the party. I would do the same. First we needed to get this loss out of our system.

I set up four regional meetings in January and February—we called them Future Forums—mostly in states where we hoped to regain our electoral advantage, or where we wanted to expand our electoral map in 2020. We'd lost Michigan, but by less than eleven thousand votes, so I planned to spread a little love in Detroit. I scheduled one in Houston and another in Baltimore. I started the tour in Arizona because, even though we lost there, we were making steady gains in that state. If the party was going to rise from the ashes, we might as well begin in Phoenix.

In each city I held a town hall with millennials, asking them what we did wrong and where we should go from here. I arranged for an inspirational speaker to open the general meeting, hoping that an uplifting message would help us expel the ghosts of 2016. In Phoenix I found that the mood was raw: angry, saddened, disappointed, and scared. I started the event telling the story of what we had been up against, but it did not seem like it was a story that people wanted to hear. People were bitter, and all of them wanted to blame the DNC. The Bernie people were saying how no one trusted Hillary, and Hillary people were complaining that the Bernie people never did come on board, even after the convention. These voters had many harsh words for how we didn't connect with folks, about why turnout was down, and the harassment that some voters had experienced at the polls. No matter how many times during these forums that I was goaded to do so, I never threw the Clinton campaign under the bus. I knew my job was to stand there and take the body blows, acknowledge it, absorb it, so that all of us could let it go.

The meetings were cathartic. I began to feel that I could end my tenure knowing I had done what I could to set things right. As I drove up to Baltimore from Washington, DC, on a cold February morning, I was looking forward to the last of these forums before heading to Atlanta for the election of new DNC officers and then on to New Orleans to celebrate Mardi Gras with my family. After the forum, the staff and I gathered at a restaurant near the Chesapeake Bay for crab cakes and beer. We were toasting each other at the moment when I felt my phone vibrate, looked down, and saw that it was Hillary.

She asked me how I was doing and I said I was fine. She sounded rested and confident, as if the Hillary I knew had returned. I told her about the Future Forums and that I felt good about the people who were running to be the new leaders of the party. We were in better shape financially than we had been in months. Before leaving the White House, the president had agreed to do one more fund-raising appeal, and our online fund-raising was outpacing previous months. We had almost $11 million in the bank, which would give the new chair a head start. This was chitchat, like I was talking to someone I didn't know. This was not *I can't wait to see you. Let's get together. You stepped up and I really wanted to thank you for doing it.* I know Hillary. I know she was being as sincere as possible, but I wanted something more from her.

The 2016 campaign, convention, and election had shattered long-standing relationships, leaving old friends wary of one another. This was more than the burnout and dejection that follows a crushing loss. The Russian dirty cybertricks that were still just coming to light had left everyone scarred and scared. We were all unable to reach out to the people we normally counted on.

As the call wrapped up, Hillary said she hoped I would be okay. That was when I almost lost it. Even if the party was starting to regain its footing, I was not okay. I had nothing left to return to. This campaign had tarnished my reputation, forced me to step down from CNN, and strained my relationships with colleagues and friends. The hacking of the DNC by the Russians shook my world, depleted my energy, creating in me a fear so deep that now I had surveillance cameras on every door and window at my house. I was struggling within myself to find a way to say this to Hillary, and if it would do either of us any good if I did, when she offered that if there was anything she could do to help I shouldn't hesitate to give her a call.

"Don't forget what happened to the DNC," I suddenly blurted out.

Words started rushing out. I summoned that strength that comes from down deep. I had held it. I had taken all the hits. Hearing her voice was the first moment I understood how tired I was of taking it. What about the Russians? They had tried to destroy us. Was she going to help? I wanted to file a lawsuit. We needed to sue those sons of bitches for what they did to us. I knew the campaign had over $3 million set aside in a legal fund. Could she help me get this lawsuit started? And don't forget the murder of Seth Rich, I told her. Did she want to contribute to Seth's reward fund? We still hadn't found the person responsible for the tragic murder of this bright young DNC staffer.

You're right, she said. We're going to get to that. But she really had to go. She had made the call and checked it off her list, and I accepted after we said our good-byes that I might never hear from her again.

In the weeks that followed, as I put my life back together, I thought about the notion that the Democratic Party is a family. I'm one of nine children, and I know how families squabble and forget because they have to move forward. They start to shrivel if they live only in the past. The other thing families are good at is keeping secrets. This Democratic family needed to stop doing that. So many things happened during this campaign that we were not supposed to talk about, and those secrets became part of our bigger problem and part of our defeat. I knew I needed to speak up. I was likely to be the first person to do so, at least in so public a way.

I wanted to tell the story of all the things that contributed to the loss, some of which we could not control and some of which we brought on ourselves. In the midst of the reality show that became the campaign, no one was focused on what was happening to the democracy, and the distractions have only continued with Trump in the White House. Amid the chaos of the new administration, the truth of what happened in 2016 is starting to slip away. We can't allow that to happen.

We were hacked by the Russians. I want to talk about what this means for our democracy. Most people are not aware of the full-scale terror it creates—fear that slows everything to a crawl as people start to doubt one another. I want to talk about the arrogance and isolation of the Clinton campaign and the cult of Robby Mook, who felt fresh but turned up stale, in a campaign haunted by ghosts and lacking in enthusiasm, focus, and heart. More than that, Hillary's campaign and the legacy project of the outgoing Obamas drained the party of its vitality and its cash, a huge contributing factor to our defeats in state and local races. I became so frustrated that in the days following Hillary's shocking collapse at the 9/11 memorial ceremony I nearly replaced her as the party's candidate for president. I want to explore the reasons why I decided not to do that and instead gave her time to heal and return to the campaign trail.

Many people don't want me to write this book. They told me no one cared about what happened at the DNC. To them, the hacking was something we would rather forget. Some seemed to think that this was only Hillary's story to tell. Others were still not convinced that the Russians were behind it. The purpose of this exhumation is to once and for all get everything out in the open.

As galling and heartbreaking as it was, the ascendency of Donald Trump to the White House has also created a tremendous opportunity for the Democrats. Once we understand exactly what happened in the debacle of 2016, we can stand up from this defeat and come back stronger.

As you can imagine, I have a lot to say about that.

ONE

Storm Clouds

As my good friend Lucy Spiegel and I drove toward the Wells Fargo Center in downtown Philadelphia on the last Monday in July 2016, we gasped at the enormous dark clouds looming over the site where the Democratic Convention would soon open. As a child in New Orleans I saw those same tall, black clouds erupt with such fury that they could bring a city to a standstill. As we got closer, my instincts were shouting at me to turn around, but we drove on. As vice chair, I was next in line to succeed Florida congresswoman Debbie Wasserman Schultz should she decide to step down as the chair of the Democratic Party. The last thing I wanted to be was the person who took her place. But suddenly that seemed almost inevitable.

The party was about to make history as it gathered to nominate the nation's first woman presidential candidate, but we were stumbling—bleeding, nearly dead from a bruising primary season. And everyone was blaming Debbie. Obama swept into office in 2008 with a majority in both houses of Congress, but in the last eight years we'd lost all of the ground we gained. We lost control of the House in 2010 and, since Debbie took office in 2011, we'd also lost the Senate and more statehouses and governorships. As Democrats started pouring into Philadelphia for the convention, Debbie did not have a lot of friends among them.

I had known Debbie for many years, and it pained me to hear her critics talk about her behind her back. I was even more pained when I joined in that chorus. I knew how hard she had worked holding down two jobs, being both a congresswoman and the party chair. One of the major complaints was that she was using her position to advance her career at the expense of the party. Calls for her to step aside started months before the Iowa caucuses and grew louder throughout the primary season during the disputes about adding more candidate debates and forums. Debbie was under fire from all sides no matter where she looked, and the Bernie people just plain hated her.

After it was clear in June that Bernie Sanders had lost the nomination, he announced he would support Hillary, but he spent the six weeks leading up to the convention complaining to anyone who would listen about Debbie and the DNC. He claimed that she put the fix in for Hillary from the start. He attacked the rules that allowed party leaders chosen as superdelegates to declare their support for a candidate independent of the results of the state primaries and caucuses. He said all the rules for the primaries had been written to favor Hillary. I have served on the rules committee since 1997, and I could assure him that the rules were not written one way or the other. The Rules and Bylaws Committee meets immediately after the presidential election is over to begin the process of writing the rules for the next cycle. The goal of these meetings is to fix whatever problems arose in the previous presidential cycle. Bernie has always been an independent, and became a Democratic candidate only for the 2016 election. Those who have run under our party rules in the past operated under them better than someone who comes from outside party politics. The Bernie folks and some other unsettled state delegations from the West were not persuaded that was the full story.

I saw these powerful divisions playing out during the negotiations over the party platform back in Orlando in the second week in July. Thousands of people had been drawn to this election for the best of reasons. In 2008 it was a time for change, but in 2016 it was a popular revolt. From the left to the right, many Americans wanted something different. That energy became concentrated on the candidacies of Bernie Sanders and Donald Trump. Their supporters worked hard for their candidates, because they believed the system needed radical reform and they wanted to have an impact. As the bruising primary campaign played out, some of their supporters came to believe that the process was rigged. In Orlando, the platform delegates who supported Bernie were outraged and wanted their grievances heard. I was hoping that as we negotiated the planks of the platform, the party could show people that we were working to make sure that everyone's voice could be heard.

I guess I succeeded a bit too well. In Orlando many delegates were inspired to make long, impassioned speeches. We had multiple drafts from different factions for each one of the platform planks. The meeting on Saturday, July 9, was supposed to be over by 7 p.m. but it went until 3 a.m., thirteen hours. As we approached midnight I had that weary feeling that we would never get out of there with all these people arguing and sermonizing. Fortunately, at around 9 p.m. I had realized what I needed, and what these people needed, was a drink.

I went next door to a store and bought $400 worth of liquor. I set up an impromptu bar and started mixing drinks and ordered food to be delivered. The hotel hosting the meeting threatened to shut me down for serving alcohol without a license, but somehow the DNC staff made that problem disappear. After a few drinks and some dinner, people were in a mood to compromise.

We negotiated a very progressive platform that both Bernie and Hillary could stand on, which I hoped would mean fewer conflicts at the convention. Still, I couldn't help but wonder why I had placed myself in this situation, though. This was Debbie's mess, not Donna's mess.

At least our convention would not be the ghoulish sideshow that the Republicans had created in Cleveland. It seemed like every prominent Republican I knew who wasn't being paid by a TV network to be there had conveniently found an excuse to stay home. In their place emerged such inspiring figures as Gen. Mike Flynn and Scott Baio. When I spotted Sen. Orrin Hatch in the convention hall, he even came up and hugged me—so relieved was he to see someone he recognized.

This was the only convention I've ever been to that literally made me sick. It wasn't just the speeches. Between the air outside, which was poisoned by the tear gas police had sprayed on the protestors, and my moldy, dusty hotel room, I ended up at the Cleveland Clinic to figure out why I was having such a hard time breathing.

The GOP convention had been so dispiriting and chaotic that I felt there was a big opening for the Democrats to build on. I knew that there would be disruptions from the Bernie folk, but our program was hopeful, and we had talent for every hour of our convention program and inspiring speakers.

I had been to nearly a dozen conventions in my time in politics, first as a delegate and later as a pundit. It was a life beyond what I could have imagined when I started in politics at the age of nine, working to elect a Kenner, Louisiana, city council candidate who promised to build a playground in my neighborhood. The councilman won, the playground was installed, and I was on my way. I've been on the staff of seven presidential campaigns, culminating as manager for Gore 2000. I have served as a strategist for more than fifty-six House and Senate races, and nineteen state and local contests. At the point when I stopped working on campaigns in 2000, I'd helped elect Democrats in forty-nine states; one more state and I would be named Miss USA without having to wear a bikini.

As I got to the end of my forties, I had come to a time in life where I did not want to be in the battle anymore. I was happy teaching my course on women in politics at Georgetown University, running my consulting firm, and getting paid to talk politics on CNN and ABC. Although I am through and through a Democrat, my decades of experience had helped me master the skill of being able to say nice things about everybody when I was on television.

I could say good things about Martin O'Malley, Jim Webb, Joe Biden, Lincoln Chafee, or Bernie or Hillary. Hell, a few times I even found a way to say something good about Donald Trump. In some ways I thought of myself as an actress, playing the part that the producers wanted me to play. In the morning when I was getting ready to go to the studio I'd know if I was going to play the part of the bitch who stands up to the GOP talking points. Or they might ask me to be the cool, calm Donna, the voice of reason and experience, who will just give it to you straight. When I looked into the TV cameras, I envisioned that I was speaking to someone older, whiter, and living in middle America who was staring at me and trying to open their minds to what this black lady had to say.

This, to me, was my perfect life: still with a voice and in the mix of politics, but no longer responsible for the outcome. I had been asked by President Obama to serve as the vice chair of the party in 2009, and I focused my attention on strengthening the Voting Rights Act. While the chair of the DNC is a paid position, the other officers do not take a salary and serve much like a board of directors for the party. I was rarely in the DNC office.

I helped raise money and worked with my staff at the Voting Rights Institute to protect the right to vote in states where it was under assault. The day-to-day operations at the DNC were in the hands of Debbie and her full-time professional staff.

The notion of being the party chair, even for a little while, did not appeal to me at all. Maybe it was just the mellowing that comes with age. I had a strong suspicion that my resistance to taking on this job was because of Kai, a little boy who had stolen my heart.

Kai was born strong and healthy late in May 2016, but the birth really tore up his birth mom, Mia. She had to stay in the hospital for six weeks with a horrible infection that threatened her life. During that time she and her wife, my best friend Betsy, asked me to care for the child. Now, I was thinking: *Here's this girl who spends all of her life guarded. Don't want no more love. Don't want no more attachments. I'm done with that. I'm enjoying my life at age fifty-six.* Then here comes this little boy who touched my heart in a way no child ever had before. Maybe this was because I cared for him and him alone ten to twelve hours a day, rather than seeing him among all the other people in a room during a visit. I fell in love. I told CNN and ABC that I needed to go on maternity leave because I did not want to be separated from Kai.

In July, after seven weeks together, I left Kai to speak in Seattle and Colorado Springs and to go from there to Cleveland to serve as a commentator on the GOP convention. I was surprised by how much I missed Kai. I rushed home on Friday after the convention to see my little Boo, even though we would only have a short time together before I left for Philadelphia. As I was relaxing with him in my arms, letting the unpleasant feeling of that GOP convention slip out of my body, I got to thinking about what a great summer we were going to have. When the days got hot, there was a piece of shade in my garden where he and I could sit and listen to the birds and look at the flowers I had planted there. In the fall, I'd bundle him up and we could see the leaves change color in Rock Creek Park. I'd still go off and do my pundit thing, but most days I could spend long pieces of time with Kai.

I was looking into those sweet blue eyes of his on July 22 when WikiLeaks dropped the bomb on the DNC.

My first sign of the trouble came when my phone started acting like it was possessed. It kept asking me for my password, and other ways to verify my identity, as if it had some kind of hardware malfunction. As that phone was not my primary mode of communication, I decided I'd deal with it later, but it would not let up. Then I got worried that I might lose the pictures of Kai I had on it because I had not backed them up. I called the tech help line at the DNC, and the man I spoke with advised me to delete my DNC email account immediately from my devices. All of my emails would be wiped out as a result. He didn't express alarm to me and never mentioned the name WikiLeaks or referenced an email dump. He promised me that the pictures would still be safe, so I would have no trouble if I deleted that account. Then at 3 p.m. the party told all the officers about the WikiLeaks dump.

On June 14 Debbie invited the Democratic Party officers to a conference call to alert us that a story about hacking the DNC that would be published in the *Washington Post* the following day. That call was the first time we'd heard that there was a problem. Debbie's tone was so casual that I had not absorbed the details, nor even thought that it was much for us to be concerned about. Her manner indicated that this hacking thing was something she had covered. But had she?

WikiLeaks had been releasing small batches of emails ever since that phone call. There were some from the DNC and

Hillary, but WikiLeaks seemed to have a grudge against everyone. It also released a few embarrassing emails from Donald Trump's campaign and Sarah Palin. Maybe these were just test batches to see how the public would react, and in truth, people were so focused on the GOP convention, these small dribbles of emails barely surfaced amid all the news.

Then came that Friday, when WikiLeaks dumped twenty thousand Democratic Party emails in a move deliberately timed to disrupt our convention.

The WikiLeaks emails—written by a wide range of DNC staff from the top leadership all the way down to the lowest employees—were carefully chosen to reveal senior members of the DNC staff speaking disrespectfully of Bernie and his supporters; one staff member had made an anti-Semitic remark. They questioned his faith and conjectured about ways to smear him for being an atheist in strongly religious states like Kentucky and West Virginia. They mocked him for being an outsider, the very thing that had energized his supporters, who were sick of establishment corruption. The emails showed the DNC staffers developing a story to plant in the press about how his campaign failed.

Suddenly you could not turn on cable news without hearing these shameful statements. There were conjectures about a convention floor fight, demonstrations to embarrass Hillary on the night she was nominated, a public display of disunity that would make the Republicans excited about their prospects in November. My inbox was flooded with messages from people complaining about the DNC's unfair treatment of Bernie. Everything we had done to unify the party was unraveling. I realized I had to leave Kai and get to Philadelphia right away.

Saturday morning I took the early train from DC to Philly. In the days before the convention opens, groups and state caucuses hold meetings and receptions, and the Democratic Party hosts meetings of the party rules, platform, and credentials committees, which are required by convention rules. The emails had cast a big shadow over these meetings, and I wanted to be there so I could try to calm things down. The party needed to go on record ASAP to apologize for the emails. I wanted to personally apologize to folks for how they reflected on the DNC, not just to the Bernie people.

As the train pulled into the 30th Street Station, I sent word to Debbie that I had arrived. I went to the Sheraton Hotel to drop off my suitcase and hailed a driver to take me to the convention center. I arrived at the convention center at ten o'clock in the morning and would stay until three in the afternoon—apologizing, it seemed, to the whole world.

First I walked right into the meeting of Sanders delegates. The atmosphere was rowdy. People were restless and looking for a target for their anger. There were no other DNC party officers there, so I got up in front of the room with the bull's-eye square on my chest.

"I'm a vice chair of the party, and I just want to say on behalf of the DNC, I'm not the chair, but I want to apologize for the nature of the emails and the conversations that you all read in the paper," I said. "I don't know much about what happened. I just got here. I came early to apologize for myself and for the other officers." I pledged to get to the bottom of what happened, but I could see that the crisis was mushrooming. The release of the emails also had exposed the personal information of our staff people and many donors, some of whom Debbie's top staff had ridiculed in their messages. The Bernie people were ready to throw bombs at the Hillary people, who were in shock as well. No one had expected this.

As the rough day wore on, we could not get any guidance from Debbie. She was nowhere in the convention hall. I called her to say that an apology should come from her, but she was defiant. "I'm not doing that," she said. If I knew Debbie, she was probably hunkered down in her hotel room trying to cut a deal with Hillary for her exit, but truth was I didn't have much time to think about that. All I knew was that the right option was to take responsibility. I went to another meeting and apologized again.

Email and text messages from journalists and the Democratic Party powerful scrolled constantly across the screen on my phone: IS DEBBIE GOING TO STEP DOWN NOW? WHEN? IS IT YOU WHO WILL REPLACE HER? SOMEONE ELSE? Finally I had to stop looking. I knew the call for me to replace her as chair was coming, but I wanted to keep my hands off it. I felt strongly that if I put myself in the center of it, a door might open and I would be the only person left in the room with no place to duck.

I wanted to disappear from view so that I could go back to being Donna. But I knew that was not very likely to happen.

The next morning, I was set to appear on *This Week with George Stephanopoulos*. From offstage, I could hear Robby Mook, Hillary's campaign manager, pretaping a segment before the roundtable. Robby was talking about the Russians, and the Russians, and the Russians, and I thought, "What does this have to do with the Russians?"

Later, when the show went live, George Stephanopoulos started asking the members of the roundtable about Robby's comments.

"First of all, this is not just a one-day leak," I said, scrambling to find something to say. "There will be a substantial number of emails that I understand will be leaked over the next couple of days, weeks, and months because it was not a one-month breach or a two-month breach . . . [The Russians] have been involved. They were in our system at the DNC for well over a year . . . Will some people have to step down, be removed, or resign? I'm sure at the end of the day, yes."

After I was finished with ABC, I rushed back to my hotel room to change clothes and put on some comfortable shoes. R. T. Ryback, the former mayor of Minneapolis and an officer of the DNC, texted: WHERE ARE YOU? R.T, who had been mentioned as a possible successor to Debbie, wanted the officers of the DNC to meet to work on issuing a formal apology from the party. I agreed.

We found a room at the convention center where we could work. Anita Dunn, who served on the Obama campaign, in the White House, and as a consultant for the DNC chair's office, had assembled a team of folks from her firm, SKDKnickerbocker, to work on the draft. She was also working with Debbie on handling the press. Hilary Rosen, my longtime friend, CNN colleague, and DNC consultant to the chair's office, was there, too.

As we sat down at the conference table, my phone was oddly quiet. Had my avoidance manuevers worked? After all my ducking and weaving away from this crisis, maybe they had forgotten me. Rumors were now swirling that Hillary was going to replace Debbie with Stephanie Schriok from Emily's List or former Michigan governor Jennifer Granholm, people who had been her surrogates. I'd be happy to help them change the rules to allow that instead of the burden falling to me. Unfortunately my fate was already written.

The first order of business around the conference table was discussing what to do about Debbie. Many people thought she should not gavel in the convention considering how much controversy surrounded her. No matter the problems many of us had with Debbie's style, she had done her very best preparing the party for this big moment. Everyone who spoke had pain in their voices. It was heart-wrenching.

As the group discussed the various options, I felt my phone vibrate. I looked down and saw it was Charlie Baker, an old friend of mine from the Michael Dukakis campaign and the chief administrative officer of Hillary's campaign.

Shit.

"I need you to come over here, Donna," he said.

"Oh no, Charlie," I said. "Oh no. Please tell me."

"I need you to come over here right away," he said.

"Oh no, Charlie," I just kept repeating. "Oh no."

TWO

From the Back of the Bus to Center Stage

As I stood to make the long walk from the convention center to the Marriott that Sunday afternoon, my colleagues knew why I was leaving. This was a somber moment. They asked if I wanted someone to walk with me, but I declined that offer. I needed to walk alone so that I could pray.

I wished my dad, Lionel, were alive. I remembered the day I called to tell him to turn on the television because Al Gore was going to make a big announcement about me. When he balked at that, I told him that Al Gore was going to announce that I was his campaign manager, the first black woman to run a presidential campaign. My father was unimpressed. He said, "It's just a job." I felt sad that I didn't have him to call now. He always reminded me to be humble and grateful, fortunate to be chosen to serve. The truth was I didn't feel lucky. I felt duty and responsibility to the party, to the president and the nominee, and to Bernie. Behind that feeling I could hear the voice of my father, a man who earned four Bronze Stars in the Korean War and always called on his children to respect their obligation to their country. I thought mostly of him during that twenty-minute walk.

Just as I was nearing the hotel I ran into Jonathan Martin, a reporter from the *New York Times*. He looked excited.

"What's going on? What do you hear?"

"I haven't heard nothing," I said. "There's so much stuff swirling."

That wasn't really a lie, but surely it was not the truth. Seemed like the job was already in me.

I walked into the huge suite Debbie had reserved at the Marriott—I think it was the presidential one—with a dining room, living room and a kitchen and big windows. She was not in tears, but she looked like she'd just stopped crying. I was tempted to cry myself, because it sure felt like someone had just died. She was surrounded by family and congressional staff, and some members of the Florida delegation, many of whom were sniffling. I looked at Charlie, but he pointed me back to Debbie. I walked over to her and gave her a hug as a hush settled on the room. Everyone was watching us.

"I just got off the phone with the president," Debbie said to me. "I spoke with Hillary. And I think all of this email stuff has become a distraction."

"Oh, yeah. I was just meeting with the officers. We're going to issue a joint statement, and I think you'll like the statement," I said.

"I want you to know I am going to step down at the end of the week when the convention ends," she said. "This is to give you some time to prepare to be the interim chair."

"That's good, Debbie," I said. "You worked hard for Hillary, and it's important that you gavel in the convention."

"You'll be the acting chair when I step down," she said.

"Just until the end of the week and then Hillary will have someone in mind," I said.

"That's not in my hands," she said. "I will step down on my terms and I will put out a statement."

"Okay, Debbie, you do what you need to do," I said. "I will always be your friend."

She still wasn't ready to resign.

"I'll be in charge of the convention and Friday I'll just turn the gavel over to you."

I left her room with that aimless feeling you get after just leaving a funeral. A major party was about to nominate the first woman presidential candidate, but this did not feel like a triumph. Hillary had more primary votes than Trump or Sanders, and all of that was getting lost because of all the damn emails.

I still didn't want to talk to any reporters. I figured Debbie should tell the world what she was up to, not me. The press loved to talk about nothing but Donald Trump and emails, and now they had a fresh batch. They loved to write about Hillary's problems and her shortcomings and never about the things that the public really cared about. This new crisis would keep us from talking about what we wanted to do for the country and how our candidate was so much more qualified and better prepared to lead than Donald Trump.

My gut told me that Debbie would not last the week. If my hunch was correct I needed to call Lucy.

Lucy Spiegel was an executive producer at CNN when I first started as a commentator for the network back in the fall of 2001. We've been friends ever since. She had retired to Annapolis in 2015, and I invited her to come to the convention as my guest so she could witness history being made when we nominated the first woman presidential candidate. I had snagged a backstage

pass for her so she could experience the drama behind this historic convention. I could get her into all the good parties. Right
then, however, I needed something from her. If I was going to be
the party chair and in front of the cameras all the time, I needed
a better wardrobe.

I already was scheduled to speak Tuesday night, and for that
occasion I had two dresses and a seersucker suit to choose from.
When you're a pundit, you only have to look good from the waist
up. I brought many nice blue tops, but down below I wore jeans
and sneakers, the perfect shoes for running around a big convention hall. I needed to step it up for this new role. With all her
years on TV, Lucy knew how to outfit me, and she was my size.
I caught her as she was getting ready to leave Annapolis, and
she threw a few more dresses that she thought I might like into
her bag. She met me at the hotel and we started to consider the
outfits. We had dresses and jewelry and shoes for every outfit
laid out on the chairs and sofas in the room, moving the pieces
around until we thought we had the right mix. I told her to buy
anything she thought I might need for the week. It was a big
relief to have my good friend take care of that for me.

On Monday morning we watched the hotel TV as the networks aired Debbie's arrival at a breakfast meeting of the Florida
state delegation. Knowing the pressure she was under, the networks decided to broadcast the ordeal live. The room was packed
with outraged Bernie supporters who started booing the minute
Debbie entered. Some held protest signs they'd printed out on
computer paper that said EMAILS and THANKS FOR THE "HELP."

Debbie was brave, a lot braver than those congresspeople
who run from the protestors at their town halls, and I was proud
of her. She stood in front of this angry crowd and acknowledged
that they were upset, but then tried to rally them to the cause of
supporting Hillary. This only made them more angry, but she
took her speech all the way to the end. She had to be escorted

through the angry crowd by security, who hustled her out the service entrance.

As I watched it all unfold on TV, I knew she wouldn't last the day as the chair of the DNC. I imagined the Hillary brain trust huddled in a hotel suite, strategizing about the phone call they would make to insist that Debbie step down immediately. I knew they would want to do this before the convention opened, so a bigger version of that caucus scene would not unfold on the convention floor and be broadcast around the world.

As Lucy and I headed toward the Wells Fargo Center that afternoon, those were the storm clouds that we saw gathering overhead, the category two hurricane that would sweep me into a job I hoped would last only a few days. I was not ready. I knew that.

"Oh, my God, Lucy," I said. "How can I just slow this down? This is happening too fast."

When Charlie called to tell me that I was to take over immediately, I told him I didn't feel ready. I wanted to use this convention to heal the rift between the Hillary and the Bernie people, but I wouldn't have time to do that if I became chair and had to run the convention itself. But it was happening immediately whether I liked it or not.

Almost as soon as I accepted the fact that I could not avoid this, it seemed everyone else knew it, too.

Suddenly I had an entourage. I had a press aide to block the media from bothering me, but dozens of other people suddenly wanted me to make decisions about one thing or another. At one point I turned around and noticed that this young woman was following me everywhere I went. I didn't know if she was a member of my staff or a stalker. I asked her who she was, and it turned out that she was Debbie's body woman, paid for by Debbie's consultants.

Her body woman?

The president has a body man, a personal aide who follows him everywhere and carries his phone and some of the things he needs, like tissues and pens; he also takes notes on things that need to be done. I have never had a body woman or man, and I found the idea ridiculous.

Finally after a few hours of her trailing behind me I realized I had to have a talk with this young woman.

"You know, this just is not going to work out between you and me," I said. "I'm sure you're good at your job; it's just not a job that I need someone to do. Let's try to figure out something else for you to do instead of following me around."

I also found out that as the incoming interim chair I was supposed to take over a room they had reserved for Debbie at the Logan Hotel, where most of the bigwigs from the party were staying. I preferred the Sheraton because it was where people I knew were staying: the party's rank and file. The community organizers and union people, the teachers and the firefighters, were all there. The Hillary people wanted me to operate out of the Logan, which had a bar called the Commons, but there were very few common people who wanted to drink there. It was filled with party powerbrokers, lobbyists and big donors, the candidate, the Secret Service, the candidate's family. Cocktails were $16 each, and a glass of wine set you back $12. Also, they didn't even serve chicken wings. Who wants to go to a bar that doesn't serve wings? The night before, when I dragged my tired self into the bar at the Sheraton after that unbelievably long day, people were shouting from many corners, "Hey Donna, whatcha drinking?" "Hey Donna come sit over here!" No one would be shouting that out at the Logan Hotel. I told Lucy to take over the room at the Logan.

The problem I faced first was who was going to gavel in the

convention. It was traditionally the role of the party chair to do so, but I didn't want to do that to Debbie. It would seem as though I was gloating in my new role, and that was so far from the truth. No matter what she did or didn't do as chair, Debbie deserved a respectful exit. I decided Stephanie Rawlings-Blake, mayor of Baltimore and party secretary, who had been intimately involved in planning the convention, would call it to order that afternoon. At 4 p.m., she did so, bringing the Democratic National Convention to order. She then turned the gavel over to Rep. Marcia Fudge, who was the permanent chair of the convention. Meanwhile I was able to stay offstage, get my bearings, and work on my speech, set for the convention's second evening.

I'd submitted my speech before the convention, but now that I was chair it was more important to set the right tone. As the convention got underway, Lucy and I holed up in my room at the Sheraton and went over my speech line by line, and we worked on picking out my outfit from all the clothes we had laid out on chairs and sofas.

I was favoring the conservative and professional choices that reflected my dutiful mood, but as the convention came to a crescendo that first night with First Lady Michelle Obama's incredible speech, I decided that I would not let these distractions and deflections get me down. We had a lot to be proud of as a party, and we could be particularly proud of Hillary and the way Bernie Sanders capped off the night with his own riveting speech.

As the first night drew to a close, I knew I could no longer be the neutral voice among the pundits. I would have to toss aside my role as the expert and get my hands dirty in this thing if we were going to win. I felt my desire to help protect Obama's legacy and accomplishments more strongly than ever after Michelle's speech. There was so much on the ballot, including Obama's protection of voting rights, criminal justice reform, expansion of Medicaid through Obamacare, and efforts to combat climate change, all of which needed to be preserved. I could not do that dressed for a funeral. For my big speech the next day Lucy and I chose a happy dress: simple black with a beautiful cream lace outer shell.

That first night felt like a miracle: After all the drama of the primary campaign and especially the last forty-eight hours, the party had managed to come together. Could we get the feeling to last through the convention? On the second night, as I strode out onto the stage, I was nervous. This was the first time in my four decades in politics I had been asked to be a featured speaker. I had rehearsed my speech so many times, but I still didn't feel as though I had nailed it. Standing at that podium, I looked out on the crowd, and it was looking into the face of America. I fell back in love with the party that had given so much to me. I searched out the Louisiana state sign, the place where I first cast my vote. I was proud to be standing on that stage to give my remarks. I felt that speech in me. I had written it myself and it came from my heart:

Growing up, I was always told that a lady should never reveal her age, so I will simply say this. I'm no spring chicken. I've seen some things in my time. And as a child, I lived through and survived the segregated south. Who dat? I sat at the back of the bus at a time when America was not yet as great as it could be. As a grown woman, I saw the first black president reach down a hand and touch the face of a child like I once was, lifting his eyes toward a better future. But I have never, ever, in all of my years seen a leader so committed to delivering that better future to America's children as Hillary Clinton.

I talked about how she did not become a corporate lawyer right out of Yale, but worked for children's rights at the Children's Defense Fund and as the first lady of Arkansas. I contrasted her life of service to the corruption and self-dealing of Donald Trump. I wanted them to know who Hillary was when no one was watching, at her core, rooting her to this earth: her hope for children and her commitment to helping them live up to their God-given potential.

My friends, as a child when I sat at the back of the bus, I was told time and time and again that God's potential did not exist in people like me. I spent my life fighting to change that, and from the first day I met Hillary Clinton I've known that she is someone who cares just as much and would fight just as hard for children everywhere. Poor kids, you've got a champion. Kids who live in poverty, you've got a champion. Kids who need help, you've got a champion. As long as she's in charge, we're never going back. And that's why I am with her! Let me say this as your incoming chair of the Democratic National Committee, I promise you, my friends, I commit to all Americans that we will have a party we all can be proud of. We will elect Democrats up and down the ballot, and we will celebrate together the inauguration of President Hillary Clinton in January 2017.

I brought the crowd to its feet with that last line. Something came over me when I made that pledge before that huge audience. I was the chair of the Democratic Party for this historic election. I felt proud of all the party had done and proud of myself for standing there at that moment, ready to work as hard as I could to bring my friend Hillary to victory. When I finished my speech, I danced off the stage, first in little steps, a bit hesitant, like I did not have my feet under me yet. As I got away from the podium and saw all the happy faces of my friends standing in the wings with their arms open to welcome me, I started to sway a little more and take bigger steps. I had a reason to get back in the fight. I wanted to win this race for my nieces and nephews and, most important, my godson, Kai. I was missing his sweet face, and those big fat jowls.

I was going to do this and do it well. I had just made that promise to the world, and it was one I hoped with all my soul I would be able to keep.

THREE

The Russians, the Russians, the Russians

I danced off the stage and right into the storm.

At the edge of the stage waiting to greet me were staff members Julie Greene and Patrice Taylor, Lucy, and Stephanie Rawlings-Blake. I was shaking from the adrenaline of making that speech, and their hugs soothed me and brought me back to center. As I looked over Stephanie's shoulder, I saw another circle of well-wishers, but they had a different motivation to grab me: money. They were donors and paid consultants for the DNC who were trying to block me from my friends and staff. The consultants had different agendas, but all were united in their desire to make sure that I didn't cancel their lucrative contracts now that I was chair. All these hands reaching out to grab me, to offer advice, to hand me lists of talking points. I shook off that crowd and went directly to see Donnie Fowler Jr., one of my "kids" and the person in charge of running the whip operation in the boiler room to tamp down signs of acrimony on the convention floor.

Taking Debbie off the stage had not healed the deep divisions
that were still tearing the party to pieces. Several of Bernie's
state delegations remained agitated, particularly California,
and the news media camped out wherever there were voices of
discord. Bernie supporters were happy that Debbie was gone,
but the system that supported her remained in place. They
would not be satisfied until there was more dramatic evidence
of change at the DNC.

Their dissatisfaction was emerging in ugly episodes on the
convention floor. I had been shocked that the Rev. Dr. Cynthia
Hale was booed during the invocation on the opening day of
the convention when she praised Hillary. Donnie, who I worked
with on former House Democratic Leader Dick Gephardt's
presidential campaign in 1988, had campaign people from
Bernie and Hillary with him in the boiler room. They had cameras on the crowd scanning for trouble. Wherever Bernie supporters would hold up signs attacking Hillary, he'd send people
to stand in front of them with bigger signs to block those people out. If someone from the Bernie faction left his seat, Donnie
would send a Hillary person as a replacement to dilute the neg-
ative energy. He used a number of tactics to calm the crowd,
and he was mostly successful. To seasoned convention watchers,
what we saw on the floor was atrocious, but most of the folks at
home saw a flawless convention, where one strong speech built
on the next, and a triumphant nominee.

Few at home or even on the convention floor understood the
pressures the staff was under independent of the angry Bernie
supporters. I was in awe of how the staff kept their eyes on
their duties while their worlds were falling apart. In the crucial
weeks before the convention, right before the party announced
the hacking, the DNC confiscated the staff's computers for the
weekend without any warning or explanation. Many people

were upset, thinking that they had been fired because Hillary's team was about to take over the party. When they got to work on Monday they found out that the cybersecurity firm the party hired had wiped their computers clean, eliminating all their files, including their files about the convention. When they asked why they hadn't been warned so that they could save important files on a thumb drive, the consultants said that they couldn't allow them to do that. If the hackers saw everyone downloading files, they'd take evasive action. No matter the reason behind this action, the staff that was working on the convention had to spend hours reconstructing all that information.

Then the WikiLeaks dump released cell phone numbers and other personal information to a hostile world. While Leah Daughtry was the CEO of the convention, Patrice Taylor and Julie Greene were responsible for many aspects of completing the party business that is conducted during the convention. They were taking hundreds of calls a day, never knowing if the call would be a death threat or a threat to their families from someone who had gotten their phone numbers in the WikiLeaks dump.

They had succeeded despite that and never complained, even when this harassment and abuse ruined a beautiful moment. I only found out later that in that happy moment when Hillary accepted the nomination, Julie felt her phone vibrate and looked down to see threats and insults from a stranger. These grotesque acts were just one element of the ugliness that was to come.

Almost as soon as I became interim chair I began to notice the ways that the Hillary campaign seemed not to respect the DNC and its staff. I had to beg the campaign to hire two buses to bring the staff up to Philadelphia to celebrate the nomination. Cheapskates. They were sitting on close to a half billion dollars in contributions and thought this small investment in morale was a waste of money. It would be a terrible slight if the staff was not allowed to share this moment. Finally I found the money to do it without approval from Hillary's campaign headquarters in Brooklyn.

As soon as Hillary and Tim Kaine were nominated, they were leaving the convention hall on a bus tour of the Midwest. Before they did, I wanted a promise that Hillary or Tim would come to the DNC meeting at the end of the convention so that they could greet and thank the staff. This is a political tradition, one that Al Gore upheld, and John Kerry, too. During the Obama administration, we could always get Joe Biden to acknowledge the staff graciously. As a former chair of the party, Tim was the one we expected would do this, and we wanted to make it as easy as possible for him. I worked with some of the other officers on crafting his remarks so it wouldn't tax his staff in any way. When Jennifer Palmieri, the campaign's communication's director, saw the remarks she got angry quick. Jennifer wanted to know who approved this change in the campaign schedule because she certainly had not.

I said I had, and I reminded her that it was customary. Tim knew this tradition and he'd said that he was happy to do it.

Jennifer glowered at me, and then at Tim's staff. Then she jumped up and walked out, slamming the door behind her.

I was thinking, *If that bitch ever does anything like that to me again, I'm gonna walk.*

How was I going to get Brooklyn to see the DNC as something more than a potted plant?

Once I got back to DC after the convention, I knew that party finances would be a top priority. I needed to know who we had contracts with, who the vendors and the consultants were, and what expenses were coming up in the next four months that I would be the chair. I asked the staff to give me an organizational chart, access to the bank statements and FEC reports, and a lesson in how the bills were paid and who signed the checks. I hadn't even left Philly yet, but I knew my other priority before that first day was to wrap my head around the hacking.

While I was still in Philly, I'd reread the *Washington Post* story from June about the hacking, surprised by how little of it I remembered. I understood why I'd brushed it aside, though. On a first read the tone of it struck me as blasé. The hacking, it said, was routine espionage. Spy vs. Spy. The U.S. government did the same to the Russians as well. These particular Russian hackers were well known, having bedeviled governments and institutions all over the planet, including the Republican National Committee and two of the presidential campaigns. At the time the article was written, all they appeared to have stolen from the DNC was some opposition research on Donald Trump, stuff that would have come out anyway in the course of the campaign. Although they'd been inside the DNC system for quite a while, the hackers didn't seem too interested in the emails and didn't appear to have collected information on the donors. The DNC had the problem handled, the story seemed to suggest. In May, even before the piece ran, the party CEO, Amy Dacey, and COO, Lindsey Reynolds, had hired a top cybersecurity firm named CrowdStrike that quickly figured out what was going on. They cleaned up the system and successfully expelled all the intruders the weekend before the story was written. Crisis solved. Or so we'd thought.

In June I thought of hacking as just another kind of theft, like if someone had broken into your home in the dead of night and stolen some of your valuables. The Chinese made off with the personal data of 4 million current and former employees of the Office of Personnel Management, where I served as a member of the J. William Fulbright Foreign Scholarship Board, in December 2014. There was even a breach inside the DNC. All candidates can use data the DNC collects on voters, but we maintain strict barriers between the campaign operations so competitors cannot spy on their opponents. In December 2015, before the 2016 primaries and caucuses began, four staffers from the Sanders campaign exploited a bug in a software update to view confidential voter data collected by the Clinton campaign. The breach caused a lot of friction between the two campaigns. So, I knew this kind of thing caused trouble, suspicion, and inconvenience, but in my experience the impact didn't last. As I reread the *Post* story, however, I saw how much more serious the truth might be in this case. The story described the hackers sneaking into the DNC in the summer of 2015, almost a year before anyone figured out they were there. They burrowed in deep and didn't make a sound. They didn't install a big, shiny piece of malware that could be detected during a routine security scan of the system. They tucked this evil thing into a vulnerability in the Windows operating software where it quietly soaked up the DNC's emails, voice mails, and chat traffic for almost an entire year.

The hackers were not two four-hundred-pound guys sitting alone in their bedrooms. They were sophisticated teams, codenamed Fancy Bear and Cozy Bear by CrowdStrike. The two bears, CrowdStrike said, came from competing Russian intelligence agencies that had teams working twenty-four hours a day to break into foreign computer systems. Pitting these two angry bears against the DNC was not a fair fight, Shawn Henry of CrowdStrike said in the *Post* article: "This is a sophisticated foreign intelligence service with a lot of time, a lot of resources, and is interested in targeting the U.S. political system. You've got ordinary citizens who are doing hand-to-hand combat with trained military officers, and that's an untenable situation."

Now this was my problem to handle. First, I wanted to talk to Marc Elias, the general counsel for the Clinton campaign. He was always well-informed, and I had grown to trust his take on things, particularly because he had helped me so much filing lawsuits for the DNC's Voting Rights Institute to oppose state attempts to suppress the vote. I needed to know everything he knew about the DNC hacking before another reporter asked me about it.

I spotted Marc at the Logan Hotel on Sunday and I walked right over to him. Marc told me to sit close so that we could talk quietly. As we sat face-to-face on couches, he started talking a mile a minute about the Justice Department and the FBI and the proof they had that this hacking had been the work of Russian agents. Marc was dropping words like *cyberwarfare*, *breach notifications*, *ransomware*, and other terms that had never crossed my lexicon.

By the time we finished talking, I must have looked like a ghost. I was terrified and confused. One thing I understood was that the hacking had not ended.

Marc also agreed that I needed to get a handle on the party finances and would likely have to begin to clean house. For that I had to talk to Charlie Baker and Gary Gensler, the chief financial officer of Hillary's campaign. Why would I need to talk to people from Hillary's campaign about the party's finances?

Trust me, Marc said, adding that Gary would clarify the situation for me so I would not be blindsided when I walked in the door on my first day in DC. Marc offered to let Gary know I would be calling. When I left Marc, I felt a little dizzy. I was starting to understand that this job I took on would be about a lot more than simply aiding Hillary in her all-but-certain path to victory.

On Friday after the convention, I took my time as I prepared to make my way home. It was a beautiful day in Philadelphia, and I was enjoying saying good-bye to the many old friends I had seen at the convention. I liked that feeling of the city emptying out, the hustle subsiding.

As I pulled into DC a few hours later, Minyon Moore was blowing up my phone with a little crisis. Minyon and I had become friends working on Michael Dukakis's presidential run in 1988, plus she was on the Executive Committee of the DNC. That evening she was packing up to move to Brooklyn to serve for the next three months as chief political strategist of Hillary's campaign. The problem was she'd locked herself out of her house. I had a key. I dropped my bags and convention swag at my house, grabbed her spare key, and was on my way to her place.

After I let her into her house, Minyon and I caught up on her front porch. How many other evenings had we spent doing just this with a glass of Prosecco? Too many to count. That night we were both on the cusp of something great. Minyon would be key to helping Hillary get elected, and so would I! Sisters in battle once again. I wanted her to tell me anything she could that was useful about the job I was about to take. I knew many of the people she would be working with in Brooklyn, but I didn't know who made the decisions. How could I be of the best use to Hillary?

Minyon said first I needed to talk to Gary Gensler.

Again with the Gary Gensler. Who was Gary Gensler?

Minyon assured me that I knew him. I'd worked with him on the platform committee.

"Was he that bald guy with the big glasses who acts like he knows everything?"

Minyon said the reason he acted like that was because he *did* know everything. Gary had been an undersecretary of the

Treasury under Bill Clinton and the chair of the Commodity Futures Trading Commission under Obama. He had worked at Goldman Sachs before he got into politics.

Not Goldman Sachs again!

I did remember working with him on the big brawl that was the platform committee. He was good forging consensus on platform planks. Gary brought me the three different gay rights platform amendments. I'd get those three different committee members together, and Gary and I would help them agree on language that was adequate for everyone, and then move on to the next dispute. I did like Gary and I knew he would tell me the truth.

Minyon, always elegant in her manners, had another delicate piece of advice for me about dealing with the smart young people in Brooklyn.

"Donna, you cannot cuss these kids out because it will shut them down," Minyon said.

"What the fuck?" I said. Damn! They picked the wrong woman for this job.

After I got home I saw that Minyon had left a case of Prosecco in the backseat of my car. I brought it inside and put a bottle in the refrigerator and called my older sister, Cheryl, in New Orleans. She was so happy to hear from me, relaying how everyone she knew in our hometown of Kenner, Louisiana, was proud of me and how much they liked the New Orleans sashay I made on my way off the stage. Oh, and how they loved my dress! She wanted yard signs, ten at least, so she and all our neighbors could show how much they supported me and Hillary. I always hesitated to tell my family that Louisiana does not matter to the Democrats in the presidential cycle. We never win that state. I didn't even know if Hillary was going to open an office in New Orleans.

There was a sweetness to the evening I relished. I had this delicious Prosecco from my good friend and a great call with my sister. I sat out in the garden chatting on the phone and batting back the bugs, sipping that Prosecco. I texted Gary and he got back to me immediately. We agreed to speak at 10 a.m.

I had a feeling that this might be the last peaceful moment before the frenzy.

FOUR

Picking the Apples

That next morning I called Gary Gensler on the dot of ten. He wasted no words. He told me that the party was broke and $2 million in debt.

"What?" I screamed. "I am an officer of the party and they've been telling us everything is fine and they were raising money with no problems."

That wasn't true, he said. Officials from Hillary's campaign had taken a look at the books. Obama left the party $24 million in debt—$15 million in bank debt and more than $8 million owed to vendors after the 2012 campaign and had been paying that off very slowly. Obama's campaign was not scheduled to pay it off until 2016. Hillary for America and the Hillary Victory Fund had taken care of 80 percent of the remaining debt in 2016, about $10 million, and had placed the DNC on an allowance.

If I didn't know about this, I assumed that none of the other officers knew about it, either. That was just Debbie's way. In my experience she didn't come to the officers of the DNC for advice and counsel. She seemed to make decisions on her own and let us know at the last minute what she had decided, as she had done when she told us about the hacking only minutes before the *Post* article about it was published online. Back in March I had emailed a friend, complaining that I hated being a vice chair in what seemed like name only and that holding a paper title was the worst decision I had made in my political career. Now I was beginning to understand how much about what had been going on at the DNC the officers did not know anything about.

On the phone Gary told me the DNC had needed a $2 million loan, which the campaign had arranged.

"No! That can't be true!" I said. "The party cannot take out a loan without the unanimous agreement of all of the officers."

I knew that was so. During the 2014 midterm Obama wanted to draw on the party's $10 million line of credit with the bank to help down-ballot races, basically putting us on the hook for $10 million of those campaigns' expenses. All the other officers said yes but I said no. Obama has no problem raising money, so he should just go out and find it himself, I said. It took them months to convince me and they did only when I got in writing a pledge that the president would help pay it all back.

"Gary, how did they do this without me knowing?" I asked.

"I don't know how Debbie relates to the officers," Gary said.

Gary was not familiar with the way the DNC was governed, but he described the party as fully under the control of Hillary's campaign, which seemed to confirm the suspicions of the Bernie camp. The campaign had the DNC on life support, giving it money every month to meet its basic expenses, while the campaign was using the party as a fund-raising clearing house. Under FEC law, an individual can contribute a maximum of $2,700 directly to a presidential campaign. But the limits are much higher for contributions to state parties and a party's national committee.

Individuals who had maxed out their $2,700 contribution limit to HFA could write an additional check for $353,400 to the

Hillary Victory Fund—that figure represented $10,000 to each of the thirty-two states' parties who were part of the Victory Fund agreement—$320,000—and $33,400 to the DNC. The money would be deposited in the states first, and transferred to the DNC shortly after that. Money in the battleground states usually stayed in that state, but all the other states funneled that money directly to the DNC, which quickly transferred the money to Brooklyn.

"Wait," I said. "That victory fund was supposed to be for whoever was the nominee, and the state party races. You're telling me that Hillary has been controlling it since before she got the nomination?"

Gary said the campaign had to do it or the party would collapse.

"That was the deal that Robby struck with Debbie," Gary said. "It was to sustain the DNC. We sent the party nearly $20 million from September until the convention, and more to prepare for the election."

"What's the burn rate, Gary?" I asked. "How much money do we need every month to fund the party?"

The burn rate was $3.5 million to $4 million a month, he said.

I gasped. I had a pretty good sense of the DNC's operations after having served as interim chair five years earlier. Back then the monthly expenses were half that. What had happened? The party chair usually shrinks the staff between presidential election campaigns, but Debbie had chosen not to do that. She had stuck lots of consultants on the DNC payroll, and Obama's consultants were being financed by the DNC, too.

Gary told me they were paying for CrowdStrike's cybersecurity services out of the building fund, not paying it out of regular receipts, thereby depleting the rainy day fund. This surely was a rainy day, but I thought we should be able to fund-raise for cyberprotection.

"Gary, I need to let this sink in," I said. "Promise me you will come sit with me and go over the books so I can see what is working and what is not."

We agreed to meet next week, but when we hung up I was livid. Not at him, but at this mess I had inherited. I knew that Debbie had outsourced a lot of the management of the party and had not been the greatest at fund-raising. I would not be that kind of chair, even if I was an interim chair. Did they think I would just be a surrogate for them, get on the road and rouse up the crowds? I was going to manage this party the best that I could and try to make it better, even if Brooklyn did not like this. It would be weeks before I would fully understand the financial shenanigans that were keeping the party on life support.

I was in a feisty mood, ready to knock over everything, but my hands were tied. Brooklyn had cleaned up the debt on our books and paid the bills, and the party should have been grateful for that, but they were not doing a very good job at running the party. The way they had stripped the party of functionality and purpose was shameful. I was beginning to understand why the campaign gave the party no respect.

I sent a message to the senior staff that I wanted to see them in the office at noon on that first Sunday after the convention. I go to St. Joseph Catholic Church on Capitol Hill, and I arrived there that Sunday morning with the intention of praying to God to give me strength and wisdom to handle this crisis in a way that would ensure victory for Hillary in November without setting fire to the Democratic Party. Before I left the sanctuary, I went up to the statue of Mother Mary and placed five dollars in the donation box. I took a white candle with me and poured some holy water into a plastic bottle to bring with me to the DNC.

I got to the office before noon on Sunday carrying a box of items I brought from home to make my office more personal. I had so much on my mind, I barely remember the drive there. When I turned onto South Capitol Street, I started to cry, but not about the situation the party was in. This would be the first time I entered the building since Seth Rich was murdered on the streets of DC on July 10, and seeing the building brought back grief about his death. He had been walking home from a local bar—and barely a block away from his apartment in Washington's Bloomingdale / LeDroit Park neighborhood— when he was shot in the back in what police said was a robbery attempt. The police were there within minutes, and Seth was still alive and talking when they arrived, but he died later that morning at the hospital.

I had just left Kai for the first time in six weeks to fly to the West Coast when I got the call that Seth had been gunned down. I started to cry when I heard the news and I had a hard time holding the tears in for the next two days. I called his parents right away to express my grief. On that Sunday after the convention, when I drove into the parking lot at the DNC, I felt that loss again. This was another thing I wanted to do while I was chair: pressure the mayor's office to find out who killed Seth Rich.

Inside the DNC building the security staff let me in, and I carried my box into the elevator and up to the main office on the third floor. I opened the door to Debbie's office and stood for a minute looking in. When she left to go to the convention, she didn't know she would not be coming back as chair. Her family photos were still on her desk and on the bureau behind it. Her orchids and her toiletries were still in the bathroom. I felt like an intruder.

This was where the staff would expect to meet me, I realized, so I walked in and set down my box. I didn't take anything out of it. It didn't feel right to stand at her desk. I sat on the sofa alongside the windows that looked at the Capitol and the Washington Monument. I breathed deep to center myself and get ready for the day. I was calmed by the beauty of the Capitol building. This was a moment for me to remember the beauty and grandeur of our country, and why we were all working hard, instead of dwelling on the pettiness and discord that was trying to tear us apart. We had a bigger enemy than each other to fight now, and we needed to put all of that aside.

I decided to call Virginia governor Terry McAuliffe for advice on getting the DNC back on its feet. I knew he'd just be getting out of church.

"Terry," I said. "I'm sitting here in Debbie's office about to meet the staff. What should I do?"

"Paint that damn office blue!" he said. I guess he didn't like her Florida pink walls any more than I did. I knew I'd keep some part of the office pink out of respect for Debbie, who was a breast cancer survivor. Many women in my family had suffered from that disease as well. Terry promised to help me solve the DNC's financial difficulties. He said that he would encourage other governors to help with fund-raising, and he offered his chief of staff to help me strategize my transition into my new role as chair.

When I called the Sunday afternoon interviews with the senior staff, I advised everyone that I wanted to learn about their duties and responsibilities. Brooklyn told me who they wanted me to fire, and some people had volunteered to leave on their own. One of the people Brooklyn wanted me to keep was Brandon Davis, the liaison between Hillary's campaign and the party.

I remembered Brandon from the convention and at first I didn't have much of a problem with him. He was a nice young man who had worked in union organizing. Patrick Gaspard, who had served as Obama's political director, had worked with Brandon in the Service Employees International Union, and had asked me to watch out for him. I'm always inclined to help a young black man on his way up the political ladder.

His title at the DNC was chief of staff, but really his role was acting as Brooklyn's eyes and ears in DC so that he could ensure that the party did not do anything that the campaign did not want it to do. No one was to breathe or to move unless Brooklyn told them it was okay. I think Debbie understood the rules of the game. She would not cause anyone any trouble. Now that I was replacing Debbie, it appeared Brandon's job had expanded to include making sure that I played that game, too.

Brandon was the first one in the door on Sunday, and he took a seat on the brown leather sofa across from me. Here was a young man without a boundary facing a woman who has walls built up and barbed wire around them, too. He was the kind of guy who would argue with you about the color of a wall. I said that this pink was too bright for my tastes, and he corrected me saying this was not a bright pink, it was a *tropical* pink. Things were not starting off well.

While we waited for the other staff members to arrive, Brandon started to tell me about all the perks that came with the office I had assumed. Did I know that Debbie had a car and a driver? That big Tahoe SUV in the garage? That was mine now.

I told Brandon I intended to sell the SUV. I could drive myself around town, as I always had.

Besides her assistant, Brandon said, Debbie had a chief of staff and a body woman. She also had media consultants and a fund-raising consultant. I was free to hire my own consultants, two or three if I liked, and bring in a new communications team. All of that would go on the DNC payroll.

I told Brandon I didn't need any consultants, and the party's communications staff was enough for me. And God knows I didn't need a body woman.

This was one way of getting the burn rate down, I thought. I wondered how many other hangers-on and sycophants were draining the lifeblood out of this party. This was the way to keep the chair fat and happy: Give her a huge staff and lots of perks and don't ask her to do anything.

The other members of the senior staff started to trickle in. I thanked them for coming in on a Sunday and asked them to wait in their offices, because I wanted to speak with them one on one. As they scattered, I saw that Brandon had remained on the sofa, as if he was going to interview them with me. Now that I was replacing Debbie, it appeared Brandon believed his job had expanded to include being my boss. This was not starting off well.

"Brandon, you have got to get out of this office so I can meet with these individuals," I said.

Brandon didn't like that very much, but he left the room.

When members of the staff came in, at first I was bristly. I had to figure out whom I could trust. My questions at first were very basic. I was filling out my own organizational chart. What do you do? What does your department do? How many staff? Whom do you report to? Any consultants working with your department?

Some of the staff gave me attitude, too. I had to be very specific in the way I asked my questions. Unless I asked the right question, I couldn't get an answer. I came to realize that I could not fire some of the people who were cagey in their responses. No matter how sneaky they seemed, they held inside them crucial institutional knowledge. It would take a while to pry that out of them. If I fired them, I would never get to the bottom of what was going wrong inside these walls.

After I had interviewed two-thirds of the senior staff—everyone except those on vacation—it was 10 p.m. I was alone in the building searching for an office I could call my own. I would never feel right taking Debbie's big office even if I painted it green, purple, and gold for New Orleans.

I found an empty office near Debbie's that had a window that looked right over the train tracks. I grew up next to the tracks, and the sound of a train passing is always a comfort to me. I brought in my box from home and took out a few pictures of Kai, one of my dog, Chip, and a sage smudge stick. I sprinkled a little holy water on the chairs and the desk and said a prayer for healing and for strength. The last thing I took out of the box was my bottle of Johnnie Walker Black.

Political veterans always remember a campaign by the vice they had adopted before Election Day. Decades ago in one campaign, my vice was Johnnie Walker. Before I left home that morning, when I was looking around for things that would comfort me in this troubling assignment, I saw that bottle in my liquor cabinet. Seeing it felt like finding an old friend in a strange town. I took one of the glasses from Debbie's bar to my new office by the railroad tracks, but I decided it was not yet time for me and Johnnie to get reacquainted.

I had learned a great deal about the dysfunction inside the party in the last ten hours. As I saw it, we had three Democratic parties: the party of Barack Obama, the party of Hillary Clinton, and this weak little vestige of a party led by Debbie that was doing a very poor job getting people who were not president elected. As I saw it, these three titanic egos—Barack, Hillary, and Debbie—had stripped the party to a shell for their own purposes. Barack never had seen himself as connected to the party. He had not come up through it the way Joe Biden and Hillary had, but had sprung up almost on his own and never had any trouble raising money for his campaigns. He used the party to provide for political expenses like gifts to donors, and political travel, but he also cared deeply about his image. Late into his second term, the party was still paying for his pollster and focus groups. This was not working to strengthen the party. He had left it in debt. Hillary bailed it out so that she could control it, and Debbie went along with all of this because she liked the power and perks of being a chair but not the responsibilities. I know these three did not do this with malice. I knew if you woke any of them up in the middle of the night to ask them how they felt about the Democratic Party they would answer with sincerity that they loved this party and all it had done for the country and for them. Yet they had leeched it of its vitality and were continuing to do so. In my three months I was going to do what I could to bring that life back.

The other thing I came to see, by listening with my heart and not just my mind, was that the perception of these staffers was wrong. With the release of the twenty thousand emails, the whole world had turned against these people. Inside and outside the party, these staffers were painted as villains. After these hours I spent talking with them, I heard the pain in their voices when they described the harassment they had endured from Trump supporters and Bernie supporters when their private email addresses and cell phone numbers were broadcast for the whole world to use. Death threats, rape threats, and vows to harm their children. Many of them had not slept well in the weeks since they became aware of the magnitude of the hacking, and that just got worse after WikiLeaks.

After speaking with them I no longer looked at them just as the million or more I needed to cut from the monthly budget. When I went home I wrote myself a big note, in big letters: "Take all the bad apples out, but remember how many good people there are here." I went to sleep after midnight, bone tired, with the knowledge that the next day, my first official day at work, would be even harder.

Remember, my dad, Lionel, had said, *it's just a job.*

FIVE

Trouble Comes to the White House

The more I learned about the hacking, the more it kept me up that night. I was frightened by all the things I didn't know and worried about how I would get up to speed quickly, now that it was my responsibility to handle this. I was not just worried about myself, though. I was worried about all the other innocent people outside the DNC who were victims of the hacking, some of whom were already feeling it, and some who would feel it soon.

I had saved dozens of emails I had received from big donors since the WikiLeaks dump that described how difficult their lives had become now that their personal contact information was available online. One donor wrote that he had not slept in days. He'd received so many threatening calls on his cell phone that he'd changed his voice mail message to a plea that people leave him and his family alone. People called to threaten him, harass him, scream obscenities, and to ask him why he was so evil. He had called the FBI, which had opened forty separate cases to investigate these calls. He, like others, contacted me to ask what the party was prepared to do.

Just that weekend, I'd gotten a notice from Home Depot that if I'd used my credit or debit card at a self-checkout stand between April and September 2014, it was likely that my identity had been compromised. The DNC had not issued a similar statement to our donors and others who had left their information on our website. Home Depot offered to repay the losses of those who had been hacked and encouraged people to sign up for a service that would monitor their online identity for fraud. If Home Depot was doing that, why wasn't the DNC?

When I got to the office the next morning, I made arrangements to interview the people I hadn't met on Sunday. Then I settled in to read the memo Michael Sussmann, one of the DNC attorneys who is a partner at Perkins Coie, sent me about the party's obligation to disclose to people that we had been hacked. So many innocent people had their personal information exposed in the hacking. The DNC site is not just for donors and party business. If someone wants to tour the White House and cannot get a ticket through their member of Congress, the DNC has a few to give out. The party also arranges for the guests at the Easter Egg Roll, and all the email information the guests furnish for those requests is entered on the DNC site. Sussmann's memo detailed how the DNC had to determine whom we had to notify.

Should we contact everyone or just those whose information we knew had been distributed? Every state had different laws governing under what circumstances and how its citizens needed to be notified, and whether or not the state attorney general should be alerted, too. The part of it that I found most alarming was that most of the states required citizens be notified within thirty days or less.

Thirty days! We'd known about this since late April, and we had not done anything to alert the hundreds of thousands of people who had placed their trust in us. Everybody was acting as if this had not happened and encouraging us not to talk about it. Hillary was enjoying a solid postconvention bounce in her poll numbers and the first positive coverage since the beginning of the campaign. No one in Brooklyn wanted to distract from the good mood with a slew of stories about the DNC hacking. Talking about these emails might confuse voters who knew that Hillary had been investigated by Congress and the FBI for the email server she kept in her home. People might conflate this disaster with Hillary's mistake. Also, Donald Trump was doing his best to conflate the WikiLeaks dump with Hillary's email server problem, and we did not want to get into a shouting match with him over it.

On July 27, the day before Hillary accepted the nomination, Trump addressed a press conference in Miami where he suggested that the hackers also had emails Hillary had deleted from her private server. "By the way, if they hacked, they probably have her thirty-three thousand emails. I hope they do," he said. "They probably have her thirty-three thousand emails that she lost and deleted because you'd see some beauties there . . . Russia, if you're listening, I hope you're able to find the thirty thousand emails that are missing. I think you will be rewarded mightily by our press." He was encouraging a hostile foreign power to commit a crime against his opponent.

While he continued to point a big red arrow at Hillary, the party had to go about the business of fixing this mess. Just thinking about the enormity of this task crushed my spirit, while at the same time I was very aware of how much I didn't know.

I needed help. While I was still in Philly I decided to set up a cyber task force of experts who could advise how to respond to all aspects of the hacking and also show me how to make sure that this did not happen again. With the help of Michael Sussmann, who had been a cybercrimes prosecutor at the Department of

Justice, I was pulling together names of people from all around the country for a conference call, where it was very likely I would not be the smartest person on the line. I hoped these experts were kind and generous people, because I was certainly going to look like a fool asking the most basic questions when we all spoke. I needed more help than just in cyber, though.

We still had an election to win, and I wanted to do my part from the powerful position I now held at the DNC. With all the new vacancies at the DNC I wanted to bring in my own team, a team that would help me help Hillary win. If we were doing hand-to-hand combat with the Russians on behalf of the party, I needed people I could rely on in a fight. There were things that the party could do better than Brooklyn could. The DNC had to take a lead on mobilizing voters in down-ballot races and in nonbattleground states. I wanted to bring on Tom McMahon and Donnie Fowler Jr.

When Howard Dean was chair, Tom McMahon had been his executive, the man who best understood Dean's fifty-state strategy—his goal to make the party viable in the red as well as in the blue states. I wanted to copy that in the time we had left before November 8. Tom and Donnie knew people in every state because of all their time in the field. I sensed we could add great value to the campaign. There is a big difference between someone from the Clinton campaign showing up who has never visited that state before, and Tom or Donnie or me calling someone they'd known in elections stretching back two decades. That kind of personal touch is the glue that holds campaigns together.

If we played this right, this campaign against Trump could increase our numbers nationwide, and Tom was someone who knew how to do that. Tom was a person with great common sense, but he also knew how to manage a crisis. I can be impatient and wanted someone who was cool when things got hot.

I've found it is smart for me to hire people who are the opposite of me. Best of all for the party, Tom and Donnie both said that they were willing to work for free. I had decided that I would not take a salary, either, as a contribution to the party that had given so much to me. I cleared away most of my speaking engagements and took a hiatus from my role as a commentator at CNN and at ABC. The only thing I refused to give up was my teaching. I learned as much from my students in the Georgetown Women's Studies department as I hoped they did from me. Teaching was a boon to my spirit. I told Julie and Patrice when they were booking events for me that the one appointment I always would make was my Wednesday afternoon class at Georgetown.

I called Brooklyn to tell them that I wanted to bring Tom on board as my executive director and that he didn't need to be paid for this.

"We care about the Democratic Party as if it is our own," I said. "He knows everybody in all fifty states, and that's what we need. He knows everybody and everybody loves Tom."

They told me no. They wanted me to rely on Brandon.

Rely on Brandon for what? He wasn't someone with superior wisdom and guidance. I enjoy learning things from those who know more than me, but Brandon had never run a presidential campaign and did not have essential contacts in the state parties. As far as I could see, he was just a clerk, the messenger who absorbed what was going on and took all that information back up to Brooklyn. Then Brandon told me that Brooklyn was sending me down a chief financial officer named Charles Olivier. *Oh no*, I thought, *now I'm going to have two Brandons*. This job was getting worse by the minute.

Monday night when I dragged myself home, I realized I had a duty to tell the other officers of the DNC what I had found in the last few days. The officers have a fiduciary responsibility to the party, and they are personally liable if it is mismanaged. What I found in the first day was alarming and I thought they should know.

I had the staff set up the call for 9 p.m. when I would be home packing for a trip to Las Vegas and New Orleans that I had committed to before I became chair and could not cancel. For the call, I was sitting on my couch, maybe a little bit anxious because I was in a state of shock. Just in that one day I had discovered so much more than my fellow officers knew, and I had to tell them everything. I told them how our big donors had been compromised and that the extent of the hacking was much more severe than the party wanted to admit. In many ways, the cyberattack on the DNC was a twenty-first-century version of the famous 1972 Watergate break-in. This time, cyberthieves broke into the party's computer server and stole confidential information. I described the party's dire financial situation and how it was being bled dry and was staggering around without an ability to lead itself out of this darkness.

In making the call it was essential for me to understand that my fellow DNC officers supported me. They told me to keep digging and let them know as I found things out.

"The sooner we get on top of it, the better we will be," said Stephanie Rawlings-Blake.

"The sooner we get on top of it, the sooner we'll know how many millions this is going to cost us," I said. We had already spent $300,000 on remediating the hacking, but I estimated $3 million or more would be the final figure.

The call lasted almost two hours. I didn't want to just deliver the bad news, I wanted each member of the leadership to have a chance to comment, to offer me advice. We needed time to express our anger that all of this had been going on and Debbie had not consulted with us. As party officials, we were stewards of the party, charged with making sure that issues were addressed promptly so that the party could survive and prosper. Although some of the officers knew a little bit about one issue or the other, none of them had understood the whole picture that I was laying out as I went down my list of issues one by one.

It was a sobering phone call, but in another way it was uplifting. Instead of making them feel like marginalized figures who were not that important to the party, I had empowered my colleagues. I promised I would keep them informed, and they promised that they would help me make these tough decisions as we continued on toward the election.

After just one day in the office, I had to hit the road. Normally I like being out in the world, but this time I had to drag myself through a trip that took me to Las Vegas and New Orleans. The whole time I was traveling, every spare minute was taken up with working on setting up the cyber task force, getting recommendations of people who might be good and willing, and calling them to see if they were available. I also arranged to be briefed at the FBI on August 11 to learn everything they knew about the hacking, as soon as Assistant Director James Trainor, head of cybersecurity, returned from vacation. I asked if any of the officers of the DNC wanted to come with me and Ray Buckley, and Henry Muñoz agreed to come along.

I got home from this trip just in time for President Obama's fifty-fifth birthday party at the White House. I'd been invited to this party every year despite the fact that my nickname among the Obama staff was Trouble. Sometimes I was good Trouble, and sometimes I was bad Trouble, but it was always something. I was sorry that this would be the last Obama birthday party I would attend, because they were always great ones. I'll never forget the time that Prince played for the president. This year it was Beyoncé who was scheduled to perform, as well as John Legend, Usher, Jennifer Hudson, and Stevie Wonder. Not bad.

The whole East Wing was packed with guests and the dance floor was full. Now I like to get out there and throw it down, pick it up, and throw it down again, but people kept pulling me aside for hushed conversations. I was outside the Blue Room when National Security Advisor Susan Rice, whom I'd known since she was a young woman in flip-flops and cutoffs working on the Dukakis campaign, took my hand. Despite the swinging party, Susan had a tight grip on me and she was staring at me sternly as she pulled me into an alcove. I remember Angela Bassett coming our way with a big smile but, when she saw the looks on our faces, she went in a different direction.

"What do you know about the hacking?" she asked.

"I don't know much of anything about the hacking," I told her. I had been spending the last few days trying to educate myself. The lawyers had talked to me, and I was reaching out to experts.

She told me I had to take this very seriously.

"I do," I said.

"It took a long time for the FBI to get any response from the party," she said. "I wanted you to know that you need to stay on top of this."

I said that I knew I had to stay on top of it. I couldn't understand why no one had taken it seriously before. I heard from Evan Perez, a CNN reporter, that the FBI had been calling and calling the DNC in the fall of 2015 to tell them that the Russians were in our system, but they never got anyone to respond. That made no sense to me. Debbie was a member of Congress. Why didn't the FBI go straight to her?

Susan said she wasn't concerned about the past. "You must promise me you will get a briefing at the FBI as soon as possible."

"I will. I have it all set up for August 11."

"Also make sure that the DNC cooperates fully with the investigators, promise me that," she said.

I was the chair now, and I could promise full cooperation as long as I held that office.

That was the assurance that Susan wanted to hear. She released me from her grip. I got the message.

I didn't know if I was going to be able to dance after that, but I wanted to give it a try. Also I wanted to be on the dance floor when Beyoncé took the stage, so I headed there. Who stopped me on my way to the dance floor but Eric Holder, the former attorney general. He grabbed me by the shoulder and led me to a less crowded spot where we could hear each other better.

"I want to ask you if you've had a chance to get up to speed on the hacking of the DNC," Eric said.

Not again! And here I was thinking that he was asking me to dance.

Yes, I said, I was moving as fast as I could to get there, but I had a lot to learn.

Good, he said. The DNC was not very responsive to the FBI. I'm glad you are taking this seriously.

I wanted to say, *How could I not take it seriously when the national security advisor and the former attorney general are ordering me to do so?* I didn't say that, though. I said I took it very seriously and was meeting with the FBI the following week. Those were the magic letters: *F, B, I.* Once I said those letters to Eric and to Susan, they knew I was in capable hands.

I got home from the party and called Ray Buckley. I felt sworn to secrecy after these direct and intense conversations with powerful figures from the administration, but I also needed someone to speak with about this. Ray is someone I trust without reservations. He, like me, is one of nine children and he came to politics early in life, just as I had; he made signs to support a gubernatorial candidate when he was just eight years old. More than that, we had worked alongside each other on the Gore campaign and still bore the scars of that defeat.

As I described to Ray the serious demeanor of Susan and Eric at Obama's party, I felt this weight settling on my shoulders. I think Ray did, too. We did not know what we were going to hear when we went to the FBI that next Thursday, but I believe we both felt that when we left that office we would not see the world in the same way that we did now.

SIX

Gentlemen, Let's Put Our Dicks on the Table

That first week at the DNC I was busy, but I was lonely. I had a notebook I was filling up with the things I needed to do or get a handle on in order to run this party. I had a page dedicated to the hacking, and at the top of it I wrote, "I need people to help me with cyber stuff." This was an area where I knew I needed outside advisors. I had a page on finances, too, and a page on party politics. I had a big staff around me, but I didn't have my crew. There were very few people with experience in the party who would understand all of these three areas. The one person who I kept aching to have on my team was Tom McMahon, but Brooklyn was still resisting the idea that I needed him.

This did not make any sense to me. How was I supposed to function as a chair and how were we supposed to function as a party if I did not have a second-in-command? There was no way that I could handle all of the responsibilities of the chair, help win the election, travel as a surrogate for Hillary, and handle the cyber attack unless I had someone at my side. I wondered if

Brooklyn was worried that I was trying to build my own power base in the DNC, but doing so was the farthest thing from my mind. The situation at the DNC was more complex than anyone in Brooklyn understood. The DNC really was like a neglected child and my job was to restore it to health. I had to help elect Hillary, preserve Obama's legacy, and rebuild the DNC. The only way I could do that was to hire Tom.

Try as I might to explain it to Brooklyn, all of my urgent pleas felt like they were words falling down a well. Take Hillary's campaign manager, Robby Mook. He had this habit of nodding when you are talking, leaving you with the impression that he has listened to you, but then never seeming to follow up on what you thought you had agreed on. At least that seemed to be the case with his interactions with me. When we would see each other, as we did many times at the convention, he was warm to me and treated me with respect, but I seemed not to be able to get a straight answer when I needed something, especially something as badly as I needed to bring Tom on board.

This was part of the removed way that he and his team encountered the world, the very quality that Minyon had warned me about that she suspected might lead to friction developing between him and me. If I was strong and made my demands in a forceful way, he was likely to flee from me immediately and avoid me in the future. The young men that surrounded Robby Mook—and they were all men in his inner circle—had mastered a cool and removed style of politics. They knew how to size up voters not by meeting them and finding out what they cared about, what moved their hearts and stirred their souls, but by analyzing their habits. They could take all the things you bought while shopping online in the last six years, analyze them, and say they were confident that they knew pretty much all there was to know about you.

If you bought a certain brand of beer and subscribed to *Golf Digest* that could predict who you were likely to vote for. Women who drove a mini van and bought romance novels and country-and-western music were also likely to vote for a particular candidate. I appreciate the importance of this data in understanding where to concentrate the campaign's resources, but what made me uncomfortable was that this microtargeting of voters brought with it the idea of small victories. They only had to persuade six people to change their votes in one precinct and twelve over here and Hillary was going to win the election.

That small focus missed the big picture, and it undervalued the emotion that drives people to the polls. You might be able to persuade a handful of *Real Simple* magazine readers who drink gin and tonics to change their vote to Hillary, but you had not necessarily made them enthusiastic enough to want to get up off the couch and go to the polls. When I interacted with Brooklyn I could not feel positive emotion behind the campaign. And I also thought my strong feelings and how I followed my gut instincts made them uncomfortable.

I was certain that Robby and his crew had the ability to identify every voter who was inclined to vote for Hillary, but in the confusion created by Donald Trump, would voters feel that their vote mattered? I was not so sure that they would. Many people in this election seemed to be voting out of spite, or out of anger, not out of enthusiasm, as if voting was a tool they were using to settle a grudge. For Donald Trump the grudge was against communities of color. If we didn't find a way to make them see that this was their election too, no amount of clever manipulation of data would bring them out to the polls.

I didn't want to criticize their method, as I knew it had power, but what I brought to the campaign was powerful, too. It was the inclusive, galvanizing feeling of sweeping up toward victory, of attaching yourself to the cause. I wanted to add that energy in the communities of color that I knew so well, in the state operations where I had so many friends. Tom agreed with me that data was a tool, but it did not solve the problem of building enthusiasm and getting people motivated. To me Tom was perfect to be my second-in-command because he had come up through the party just like I had. He had a deep love of its traditions and history. He knew we were not just a building, we were an institution. Despite the attempts by Robby and the rest to strip the party of its functionality and independence, Tom knew what a huge contribution the party could make when it was strong and healthy. And he knew dozens of important people in every state, often the same people I did, and a few more. I could say to him, "Get Fred in Arizona to do that." He'd know precisely who I was talking about without needing a last name and was likely to have Fred's number in his phone already. With him at my side my burden would be lighter and everything at the DNC would go more smoothly.

Brooklyn didn't want people who could second-guess them, people with more experience. To me, this seemed foolish because you need people who have those kind of connections to get things done and also to inspire the base. Everybody worshiped the data and the analytics. And I worship the people, the people who made politics what politics is. It's like if you had a bunch of great chefs in the kitchen and you're all trying to make the perfect gumbo. And Robby was like, "Let's just get it online. We'll order it from the best gumbo place in Louisiana." He was arguing with me as to whether or not you need a roux. You know what? You need a roux.

I had asked nicely about hiring Tom but that nice try had been ignored. I had gone around Robby to get allies in pleading my case that hiring Tom was not just important to me, it was vital to Hillary's victory. A week into my job I was beyond frustrated, and my thoughts returned again and again to the idea that if I was going to get action, I needed to be so direct that no one would ever forget what I was asking.

There's a part of my personality that I don't like anyone to see, a part of me that is my Daddy's girl. I call her Dolores and she does not like it when she thinks people are not being straight with her. I don't want anyone to see Dolores but I could feel her rising up inside me as Brooklyn continued to waffle about Tom. One night when I went home I called Charlie Baker to warn him that I was struggling to keep Dolores contained. "Charlie, I'm about to kill Robby," I told him. "And it ain't going to be pretty." Charlie told me just to get Robby on the phone and he'd help us reach a compromise that would get Tom on my team.

The next day I brought Patrice, Julie, and Brandon with me into the chair's office and placed the phone at the center of the table to dial into a conference call to Brooklyn. On the other end of the line were Robby, Charlie Baker, Marc Elias, and Marlon Marshall, who was Robby's lieutenant and the director of state campaigns and political engagement. Marlon had also worked on the 2012 Obama campaign as deputy national field director. I announced that I wanted them to explain to me what the problem was with hiring Tom McMahon as my chief executive officer.

Robby said I needed to wait for the campaign to decide if it wanted to spend money on hiring a temporary CEO.

"What?" I said. "You don't have to spend money on him. He said he'd work for free. That can't be your reason. Tell me straight."

There was an awkward few seconds of silence before Robby said that Tom had to be properly vetted.

"Oh come on!" I said. "What's the problem with Tom? Tom has a great reputation. People love him. The press loves him."

Charlie excused himself and said he had to go off the call for a minute, but I pressed on.

"If you don't want to call him the CEO, call him the transition director," I said. "I'm sure that the title doesn't matter to him. We're way past that stuff. Everyone in this party knows Tom. He's the one person in this organization that does not need to be vetted by anyone."

There was some shuffling on the other end of the line about how, yes, everyone loved Tom but the campaign wanted me to "try to work within the existing staff parameters." At that moment, Dolores showed up.

"Wait a second," I said, with my Dolores rising. "It was OK if I was going to keep Debbie's staff or her consultants, but I cannot get someone to help me run this party? Even someone who is willing to work for free? Someone over there is lying to me."

Charlie announced himself back into the call. He said he'd just vetted Tom and that Tom had passed, even though Charlie had only been gone for a few minutes. Great, but I was not done yet.

"Folks, I want us to be ambitious. We have so many tools at our disposal," I said. "Let's think as big and bold as possible, knowing we might fall short, but it will not happen because we didn't plan for a better future. We need a grassroots plan to encourage donors to reinvest in our work. Before you empty the building at the end of August, let's pull this plan together and make it count and bring Tom on board."

Brandon seemed to think that this was his call, so eagerly was he parroting the statements of his bosses in Brooklyn. They didn't have the money for me.

"This is not a sustainable system you have me operating under here," I said. "I can raise money for the DNC but I cannot control it. You control all the money and I have no say whatsoever in how it's spent. We are being attacked every day by cyber forces that want to bring our party down, and I need money to ensure the integrity of our operation. You're stripping the party to a shell. I have no ability to act to defend it."

I have worked with men all my life in politics and I can sense when they get to this part about not being able to deal with a woman. This was not a racial thing. This was a gender thing. Every time you mention that they are trying to shut you down because you are a woman, all these guys are like, "No, no, no." I would not say that, and I would not act like someone who was asking for permission. I had given them all the logical reasons why I needed Tom on board. I had run out of rational arguments.

"Y'all are thinking I am going to back down from this fight. No. I am not. We're just trying to preserve the DNC—the DNC is a wreck. We're just tired of just plugging up the holes of this leaky party. Tom knows the building. He was there when we won the presidency in 2008 and took back the House and the Senate, and besides, our CEO is gone."

Of course Brandon agreed with the men in Brooklyn. He looked at me sternly as if it was annoying him that I would try to take back control of the party as any chair would. Dolores was becoming furious.

"You know, this does not feel like a negotiation to me," I said. "This feels like power and control. Gentlemen, let's just put our dicks out on the table and see who's got the bigger one, because I know mine is bigger than all of yours."

The sound on the other end of the conference call was a rustle of confusion.

"So what will it be, gentlemen? Because I am not waiting around anymore for permission. What do you say?"

After some more deflecting and dissembling, their response was that they would have to get back to me.

When the call was done, Brandon left the room, looking disgusted. This day was serious. This whole election was serious, and for a moment there I was concerned that I had taken it too far in the way I had confronted Brooklyn. I recovered from that quickly though. We could not lose this election to Donald Trump and I was not going to play nice or waste time. Dolores might be rude and feisty, but she usually got what she needed. Those boys in Brooklyn probably never wanted to speak to Dolores again.

By the end of that day, I got a message that Brooklyn had agreed to allow me to bring on Tom McMahon.

SEVEN

Meeting at the FBI

Back in the office on Monday of my second week on the job I had to work quickly and with focus, because I was scheduled to leave for another trip to New Orleans that night to attend the Progressive National Baptist Convention. If we were going to fight this cybermenace and help win an election, we needed more money in the bank. I had taken a look at the budget, and there were a few easy places to trim back. One was consultants. The DNC had two political consulting firms who were getting paid $25,000 a month: Hilary Rosen and Anita Dunn via SKDKnickerbocker and another firm headed by Jen O'Malley Dillon, the co-founder of Precision Strategies. Love you ladies, but the gravy train has reached the last station. I also needed to talk to the president about his $180,000-a-year pollster, too. The outgoing president no longer needed to assess his approval ratings or his policy decisions, at least not when the Democratic Party was fighting for its survival against a hostile foreign power. I knew, however, that even with all these cuts we still needed more money if the DNC was going to make an effective contribution in the final three months of the campaign.

We also needed to find a way to talk about the hacking of the DNC that did not reflect poorly on Hillary. I understood the campaign's focus on crafting a better, more positive message for Hillary, and highlighting the hacking was not going to help her there. Yet if we didn't talk about the hack, didn't explore its implications, we could not make progress in getting the rest of the country to see how serious this was.

One of my friends, a former Democratic strategist, had moved to the private sector and was working at a company that had been hacked in a similar way to the DNC. I called him for a chat and found him eager to help me. He gave me a new way to talk about this. When the emails are released, the press and the public are titillated by the content in the emails, and that is what gets all the coverage. His company was embarrassed and playing defense on that, as the DNC was still. What gets lost, he told me, is that this is a crime and should be treated as such. When everyone is busy snickering they cannot get outraged at the violation. We needed to try to turn the public's attention to the crime and the need for a concerted effort to increase cybersecurity.

Amen to that, but in this crazy election, how could we break through the noise?

He suggested we have prominent Democrats write op-eds for major newspapers about the hacking and to take this message on television, too. Also, couldn't the Democrats propose legislation to strengthen our cyberdefenses? Doing so would be a constructive way to show we were learning from the experience and trying to help others, too.

These were very good ideas. As I was jotting down notes about what he said, and asking him to send me a memo, I had my doubts. I feared that even with such positive suggestions I would not be able to get anyone in Brooklyn to listen to me. Then I thought of Brandon. Was there a way to make him useful to the DNC? Although Brandon saw himself as a power broker, he rarely stayed in DC long enough to build a power base. The staff told me that once or twice a week, without telling anyone, he did not show up to work. The next day they would discover that he had been up in Brooklyn reporting to his handlers. Unless you're in the room when things need to be decided, no one under you is going to seek your guidance. I could live with him reporting to Brooklyn, but I was an officer of the DNC and its chair. Robby should be taking my calls. I didn't want Brandon's guidance. I wanted money and he was just one of the levers I planned to pull to get it.

I called Brandon into my office because I had decided the minimal amount of money I would need to help supplement Brooklyn's efforts on the ground to win this election was $10 to $12 million. Immediately he said I would never get that so I revised it down to $8 million. I didn't just come up with this figure on the spot. I had analyzed past DNC expenditures during presidential campaigns and believed we needed to spend more money on media, literature, and surrogate travel in nonbattleground states like Arizona and Georgia. I was also concerned about the U.S. Senate races and down-ballot contests in Illinois, Indiana, and Missouri. Also I thought it was a good time to try to renegotiate the terms of our relationship. Brandon and I had not started off well, but it was still early. He came into my office with a slightly bemused look on his face, as if he was coming to visit a crazy, senile old auntie and couldn't wait to tell all his friends the nutty things she said.

"I don't know who you are. You are reporting to Brooklyn. I need someone who is thinking about the party. Brandon, I need $8 million from the campaign, so let's figure out how we're going to get that."

Brandon's brows jumped higher and his eyes widened. He told me no. There was no way I was going to get that. He would not take that request to Brooklyn.

"It's not a request, Brandon. The DNC needs $8 million to help Hillary win this election. I thought I'd start with you, but I'm going to go around you shortly after you leave this room."

Brandon stiffened in his chair and his bemused look fell to seriousness. He told me that he represented the campaign and he spoke for Brooklyn whether I liked it or not. I could go around him or above him, but the answer would be the same.

I was boiling inside at the arrogance of this young man. Did he not understand that I had long-standing friendships with most of his superiors in Brooklyn, with the exception of Robby Mook? I had the cell phone numbers of people he was still calling "sir" and "madam." This was me being nice, but it was not going to last for very long.

"You know, Brandon, I want to have a black-on-black conversation with you."

He looked so startled it was as if I had slapped him in the face.

"What are you here for? What is your purpose in life? Why do I need you? I have never needed a liaison or a translator in my life. I am the chair of the DNC and as far as I can see, you are nothing more than a clerk. Take that message up to Brooklyn next time you sneak off up there. Tell them the chair of the DNC doesn't make requests, and she doesn't talk to clerks."

Brandon stood up, rattled by my directness. He was insulted but he had not let loose the idea that there was something just a little bit crazy about the chair of the Democratic Party. When he left, I wondered who in Brooklyn he called first to report about the madwoman of the DNC.

When I went home, I called Ray Buckley while I was packing for New Orleans. I realized this was becoming a habit with me and that I was getting to be a bit dependent on it. A former state legislator in New Hampshire, Ray is the chair of the New Hampshire Democratic Party and one of the biggest political power brokers in New Hampshire. Ray is also a steady person. He never reacts too strongly, but he never underreacts, either. His memory is first-rate and he rarely forgets anything you tell him. I guessed I'd found my therapist for this election.

The Progressive National Baptist Convention in New Orleans was great, but on August 10 I was desperate to leave. There was a once-in-every-five-hundred-years storm coming. My first flight had been canceled, and it looked like they might do the same for all the flights heading east through the storm. If I didn't get out by 6 p.m. there was a good chance that I would not be back to DC in time for my FBI briefing on the morning of the eleventh.

I was standing at the airport in a frenzy as I looked at the black clouds through the big windows in the waiting area. Always with the clouds! This was not just one big storm like Katrina or Sandy, but a bunch of medium-sized thunderstorms getting together to drench the earth with as much moisture as a category four or five hurricane. A truer metaphor for this election would be hard to find. People outside hurricane country don't seem to take this kind of storm seriously because it doesn't have a name, but I took it seriously. In order to escape this metaphor, I had to book a flight to Dallas-Fort Worth and then on to DC. The plane shook something awful as we ascended, and I was beginning to question if all of this was worth it when we finally broke through the edge of the storm. We had a smooth flight the rest of the way to Dallas, and I was back home and in my bed a little after midnight.

The morning of August 11 I drove down Ninth Street to FBI headquarters. I'd been a resident of DC for more than thirty-four years and never had I been to the FBI. My assistant Ro'chelle Williams, from my consulting firm Brazile and Associates, met me around the corner from the Bureau and took my car to my downtown office. The last thing I wanted was a parking ticket outside the FBI.

In the lobby I met up with Ray and Henry Muñoz from the DNC and Tom McMahon, whom I had just been able to bring on board. When Michael Sussmann arrived, he took out his security clearance badge, likely left over from his time at the Department of Justice. I was impressed. And Shawn Henry from CrowdStrike, our cybersecurity contractor, came right behind and took out something from his backpack that got him through the first screening.

Proudly I took out my top security badge from the State Department and flashed it at the window. The man there told me that it was not a sufficiently high clearance for the briefing we were about to attend. I wanted to be with the crowd that just had to flash their badges, but Ray, Henry, Tom, and I had to fill out extremely detailed forms just to be let in the building.

To get to the briefing room we had to go through a security screening just like the airport TSA's, only we had to turn over our phones and all our other devices. After we handed over our electronics, we went through another screening before we crossed the atrium and entered a different part of the building. At that entrance, there was yet another screening before they ushered us all into a windowless room and handed us forms to fill out.

While we were filling out the forms, a staff person told us that we were being videotaped. Then she read aloud the warning at the top of the form that said if we revealed to anyone what we discussed with the FBI, we would be committing treason. They had taped us listening to her read this so that there could be no ambiguity about what we had pledged to do.

Assistant FBI Director Trainor greeted Michael Sussmann warmly and introduced the other people he'd brought with him. All I can recall is everyone had a long title with the word *cyber* or *counterintelligence* attached to it. I wanted to make small talk, crack a joke or something to bring a little humor to the room of humorless people, but Trainor placed himself directly opposite me at the table. This was not the moment for joking. As the agents described the Russians' methods and the extent of the cyberattacks in the United States, not just in the political sphere, I was so scared I wanted to walk out the door and flee the country.

All my life, I have binge-watched crime dramas and love movies with cops being the heroes, but this wasn't a movie. This was real life and it was happening in real time. At the conclusion of the two-hour meeting, I wanted to tell the taxi driver not to take us back to the DNC but right to the Pentagon. This was a war, clearly, but waged on a different kind of battlefield. During that twelve-block ride up Capitol Hill, we didn't say a thing. Henry looked left, Ray looked right, Tom was checking his phone, and I was in suspended disbelief looking straight up at the dome of the U.S. Capitol.

As soon as we got back into the building, we sat numb and silent on the couches in Debbie's office. I am not one to tremble, because I am my daddy's girl and I do not scare easily. After that meeting I was just looking at the sky wondering what it was that we should do. Patrice kept walking in and out of the office, but no one wanted to talk or take our order for lunch. Patrice told me later that we looked as if all the life had been drained out of us. I finally asked her to leave so I could talk to Tom, Ray, and Henry. My first words were, "What the fuck!"

Ray said he half-expected that Jason Bourne was going to come flying through the wall when we were being briefed. We all started to laugh, which was good.

"Donna, if God forbid I was ever appointed to the Senate and told that I was going to be on the Intelligence Committee, I would resign," he said. "There is something to living in a world where you just don't know."

We had a conference call with the other officers, and I struggled to hint at the things we could not describe. It was heartbreaking to see how so much of what we had been told could happen or might happen would now actually play out. Now I appreciated why I had chosen Ray as my confidant. He and I had shared this experience, and no matter what would come in the months ahead he was someone I knew I could rely on. I would talk to the cyber task force at our next phone call about how this information from the FBI might help us focus our plan on what to do next, but no matter what that plan was, I would always be able to depend on Ray for emotional support.

This day was serious. This whole election was serious. I didn't want to talk to anyone. When I went to my office by the railroad tracks I pulled out my bottle of Johnnie Walker and poured myself a nice stiff drink.

EIGHT

The Duck and the Spook

By the third week of August Washington clears out. Members of Congress are home for summer break, and all the Washington players and their staffs plan vacations then, when the DC weather gets thick and swampy. Traditionally that's when Democrats set out their beach towels on the sand at Martha's Vineyard. In the summer of 2016 President Obama and the Clintons were among the vacationers there. Reluctantly, so was I.

I never did understand why almost every big muckety-muck in politics ended up on this little island off the coast of Massachusetts where upscale black professionals have come every summer since the turn of the last century. I never felt I fit in there, among the black elite. I like a dock on a lake, a boat to go fishing, and a loud band in a dive bar at night.

What brought me to the Vineyard was a panel I was scheduled to appear on called "Race and the Race to the White House." It was sponsored by the Hutchins Center for African and African-American Research at Harvard and would feature Henry Louis Gates and Charlayne Hunter-Gault as moderators and *New York Times* columnist Charles M. Blow among others on the panel with me. Glenn and Debbie Hutchins invited me to stay in their house in Edgartown.

If I was interested in escaping politics, the Vineyard was not the place to go.

Glenn was playing golf with President Obama, while Hillary was working nonstop raising money. She and Bill were going to afternoon barbecues and nighttime clambakes, any place where the donors might be gathering. I was impressed with her energy. I heard about her comings and goings from my sweet little guest apartment at Glenn's place, where I was hoping to tune out the world of campaigning.

Truth was that I was as eager to get out of DC as everyone else was. I wanted to shake off that frightening FBI briefing by getting far away from its shadows. By the middle of the month, I had sent all the letters to inform our donors and others, as required by forty-seven states, about the cyberbreach at the DNC.

After our meeting with the FBI, I appreciated what Ray said about wanting to live in a world where you didn't know all the terrible things that were happening around you. Unfortunately, as the chair of the DNC, I could not live in such a world. I knew I could not tell anyone what we had heard in that briefing, except for the fact that the Bureau was certain that this cyberattack had not stopped. If Cozy Bear and Fancy Bear were still trying to penetrate the DNC computers, my mind spun the various other nefarious ways they might be trying to mess with our democracy and throw the election to Donald Trump. Were there spies on the streets following our staffers? Were there moles inside the DNC building? Now that I was the chair, did they have their sights set on me?

In the days before I left for Martha's Vineyard, I could not seem to get away from the crisis that had started at the convention and continued through the month of August. Every night when I went home Patrice Taylor, the DNC's director of party affairs, gave me a list of people to apologize to about the hacking. I'd start around 7 p.m. when I opened a bottle of wine and sat on my couch to dial, starting with the people on the East Coast and moving west across the country with the setting of the sun.

I had my apology speech down to about ten minutes. *I'm sorry that it's taken so long for me to call you and apologize for the fact that your data was compromised. We are going to do everything we can to protect your identity in the future. We're going to notify you officially as is required by law, but the party is taking extra steps to make sure that this does not happen again. I've created a cybersecurity task force, and our system is up and working again. I want you to know we have not just put a Band-Aid on this, but a tourniquet to make our system safe going forward. And again I want to apologize for all the trouble that we have caused you and your family.*

Most of the donors I contacted were grateful that I called, so I kept doing it, putting in fourteen-hour workdays, in the hope that this personal touch from the party chair would make them less inclined to sue us. It was exhausting to end every day this way, but it was important, and it was sincere. By the time I left for Martha's Vineyard, we estimated I had apologized to four hundred big donors.

In the week after the FBI briefing and my "Gentlemen" outburst on the conference call with Brooklyn, Charlie Baker and Minyon Moore from the Clinton campaign came to town and we had lunch. I wanted to explain to them my vision for what the party could do to help build enthusiasm for a Hillary win, if Brooklyn would only let loose of some of the money that was washing through the DNC.

The campaign was raising millions of dollars through the DNC, and because of the agreement they had made to pay off the party's debt I could not touch a cent. The states were raising money, too, but that money was not under the states' control, either. All of this was in the hands of Robby Mook, who wanted to maintain control of all the funds and spend them in the way that he saw fit. Hence Brandon dogging my every step, to see to it that I did not get some crazy idea that I could be independent and follow my instincts about what the states needed and when. I chafed against these restraints, and it offended them when I expressed this frustration. This was confirmation of what I had gleaned from my interactions with Brooklyn. They did not like the fact that I trusted my gut and made decisions based on it.

Their focus in Brooklyn was raising a billion dollars to get to the 270 electoral votes needed to win the election. They were less interested in helping the down-ballot races unless the money flowed through to the Democratic Senatorial Campaign Committee and the Democratic Congressional Campaign Committee to elect members of Congress. Brooklyn's idea seemed to be that the coattails of Hillary's victory would sweep all the grateful candidates into office as a great wind was at the party's back. I knew enough about the grassroots to understand that was a myth. The candidate at the top benefits from the energy at the bottom of the ticket, the state and local races that build excitement, a sense that we are all part of the team that is sweeping forward to victory. If you neglect those races, not only do you lose an opportunity to foster the next generation of candidates, you just might lose the whole damn election.

Over lunch, Charlie and Minyon said that I should take this up with Robby, but I knew that would not be a good conversation. You know, you cannot leave me in a room with a bunch of smartass white boys for ten minutes before it all starts to go wrong. I knew Charlie and Minyon heard me, but it was also clear that there was not much that they could do.

The hacks and the DNC's finances weren't my only problem. I just escaped the massive storm that drenched my home state when I flew to Dallas on that night of August 10, but in the week that followed I was dealing with the aftermath. On the eleventh the storms gathered in the area around Baton Rouge and Lafayette and hovered there for eighteen hours. The torrential rain of two or three inches an hour dumped three times as much water as Katrina had. Thirty-one inches of rain fell in a single day. The weather service said in all the storm had released 7.1 trillion gallons, enough to fill Lake Pontchartrain about four times; Katrina had drenched my home state with 2.3 trillion gallons.

Most of my family is in Louisiana. Katrina changed their lives. Some ran, some had to be rescued, and all of them were displaced. I felt a huge responsibility not just to help them but to help the state. Gov. Kathleen Blanco asked me to be part of the Louisiana Recovery Authority, and during those years I was in and out of the Bush White House as often as I had been when Bill Clinton lived there. I felt a moral obligation to help the entire people of Louisiana, not just my family, to rebuild. Eleven years after Katrina, when the state was getting back on its feet, here was this no-name storm to knock it back on its heels again.

So while I was supposed to be relaxing in the comfortable rocking chairs on Glenn's porch on Martha's Vineyard, I was on my phone and iPad communicating with FEMA and with the president's staff about the record flooding in Baton Rouge, making sure that resources were going to the places where they were needed, and fielding calls and messages from hundreds of people in my extended circle who were trapped or displaced by the flooding of ten rivers. And into the middle of all this walked the Damn Duck.

Evidently someone in a Donald Duck costume kept showing up at Donald Trump's campaign rallies calling him out for *duck-*

ing the release of his taxes. *Ha ha*. With all the noise and confusion and flat-out fear of this campaign, the duck did not surface to the level of my other concerns until one of my bosses at ABC emailed me. The message was titled, "I hate to bother you on your time off . . ." and it read: "BUT—Richard Bates of the Walt Disney Company is trying to reach you about the DNC's using Donald Duck. He is desperate." Then the phone rang, and it was Robin Sproul, the DC bureau chief from ABC News.

"Donna, you have got to stop using the duck," she said.

"What do you mean?"

"Well, the Clinton campaign and the DNC are using Donald Duck at these Trump events," Robin said.

"No we're not. I didn't approve that," I said.

I looked online to see what she was referring to and suddenly I was seeing that duck everywhere: in Los Angeles, in Charlotte, North Carolina, and even one going down the escalator in Trump Tower, just as the other Donald had to announce his candidacy. This duck got around! The Damn Duck was even issuing press releases, questioning if Trump was not releasing his tax returns because he was not as rich as he was claiming to be, or didn't really donate to charity, or didn't pay any taxes. And press reports said that Donald Duck was from the DNC, intending to follow Trump wherever he appeared to heckle him for not releasing his taxes.

I sat on the porch at Glenn's looking out toward Katama Bay, stunned by the idiocy of whoever thought this was a good idea. I have never been a big fan of people dressing up in animal costumes to make a political point. This was not the Macy's Thanksgiving Day Parade and it was not Mardi Gras, either. I'd been chair for less than a month, but I thought I'd taken control of all these different factions and finally calmed things down. Here was evidence that I still had to resolve many ongoing things lest the party continue to be embarrassed by these amateur stunts. Donald Duck is owned by Disney, which owns ABC. In addition to all the other trouble the party was in, we just might have a trademark infringement case on our hands. I had to stop the Damn Duck.

"A duck?" I said to Glenn Hutchins. "How the hell did a duck get past me?"

So I called Patrice at the office. She said she would have someone from the press office call me, because they had been coordinating it.

"You mean we have a duck?" I asked. "We have a duck! Why do we have a duck?"

I hate the duck. When I was a kid people used to call me Daffy because my name was Donna. I don't want no damned duck, and now Richard Bates, the ABC vice president of government affairs is calling me. I called the DC office again.

"Kill the damn duck!" I said. "Kill the fucking duck, goddammit!

"Why are you worrying about the duck?"

"I hate the duck!"

The idea that the campaign—and as far as I knew it was not the DNC—was paying someone to follow Donald Trump around in a duck costume struck me as the opposite of what we should be doing to keep the focus on Hillary's strengths as a candidate. And, by the way, was this not proof of paid protestors? Every time Donald Trump made the claim that we were paying people to protest his rallies, we denied it furiously. That was just not something that the Democrats would ever do, and then here was the Damn Duck. I started emailing up the ladder at the campaign to get to someone in a decision-making role to fix this, but the first person to respond was Brandon.

Brandon said this was no problem. The campaign and DNC lawyers had signed off on it and besides we had not heard anything from Disney.

The reason I was emailing was because we *had* heard from Disney.

I was sitting on the porch of this beautiful home hearing the soothing sound of the ocean just a few hundred feet away but I was spending all my energy on this duck. Glenn was part owner of the Boston Celtics, and inside the house in the kitchen were three very fine-looking basketball players making me breakfast, and I was out here where the WiFi signal was best, trying to get someone to pay attention to the risk posed by this Damn Duck. I was supposed to appear on that panel about the presidential race in a few hours, but I could not settle in and focus on the comments I was going to make. Who could I get to kill the Damn Duck?

By the afternoon I had made some progress in convincing some of the campaign leaders and lawyers that the duck had to go, so I could concentrate on making my case for Hillary at the panel, but the duck was always in the back of my mind. I sat at the front of the Old Whaling Church in Edgartown, my iPad on the table in front of me so I could follow the updates the Obama administration was sending me about its response to the storm. I was in touch with the governor of Louisiana and the mayor of Baton Rouge as well as with FEMA. In between notifications from them, I was getting distracted by messages about the Damn Duck.

By the next morning I got a call from Charlie Baker wanting to know why I was worried about the duck.

"Charlie, because I'm still—I'm on leave from Walt Disney, which owns ABC. I'm an ABC contributor, and it's their duck. Not my duck. Not the DNC's duck. It's their duck and they do not want us to use the duck. Please stop using the fucking duck."

I hung up the phone and looked online where I saw they were using the duck at a noon Trump event.

I'm slow to anger, very slow, but once I am angry, get out of Delores's way. I called Marc Elias, the lawyer for the Hillary campaign, and told him that I had heard from ABC and Disney about the duck and he had to kill it.

"The duck is the intellectual property of Disney. They could sue us, okay? Do you want that story out there? Hillary's about to go to California to raise money and she's going to see Bob Iger, the CEO of Disney, who is holding this fund-raiser, and this is coming from him. What do you want to do? Have him cancel the fund-raiser? I know you all want that money. So get rid of the fucking duck!"

"Donna, this was Hillary's decision to use the duck," he said. He explained a close friend had suggested it to Hillary and she thought it was a great idea. Apparently someone wanted to use Uncle Sam but Hillary's friend vetoed that, saying a duck was a lot funnier.

Was he kidding? He was not. *What a brilliant decision! Can someone get this message to her? Is she the only one who can kill the Damn Duck?*

Marc Elias was the man to call. By noon he had killed the duck once and for all, and the next morning I was able to enjoy my breakfast with the NBA. I enjoyed it very much, in fact.

After breakfast I was sitting on the porch with Glenn getting his advice for how to deal with the constant cyberattacks and the lack of response from Brooklyn. Meanwhile I was happy to see that the problems in the Trump campaign were all over the news. Trump's campaign manager, Paul Manafort, had been forced to resign due to his questionable ties to Russia and Ukraine. In politics, when a campaign says that such and such a thing has become a distraction, what they mean is that the person is a liability. Manafort, according to an investigation by the *New York*

Times, had taken nearly $13 million from a pro-Russian political party in the Ukraine to help swing the election its way. For all of Trump's finger-pointing about "Crooked Hillary," he had ethical issues of his own in his campaign, and they were tied to the Russians. Wait a minute, I thought. The Russians were in Trump's campaign operation, too? If they were, it seemed they were not operating in the same way they were in the DNC.

As distracting as the development was, I had donors to meet. That was my other task on Martha's Vineyard. I was doing the grip and grin, meeting in advance with donors before Hillary arrived to get the audience excited about the campaign. They all wanted a personal update from a party leader about what was going on inside the campaign

Here's how these events work. As you stand in this beautifully groomed backyard next to huge platters of steaks, lobsters, and clams, you get interrogated by the high-dollar donors who pepper you with questions about what the party intends to do about the issue they consider to be the most important. How you respond to these questions about climate change and the Trans-Pacific Partnership determines the amount these donors will give. These are smart people who know a tremendous amount about the subject they're questioning you on, so you cannot give vague answers. You have to be on your toes. You also have to look confident and casual and show that you are not manipulating or hiding anything.

After I did my warm-up act, the crowd was prepared for the arrival of the star. Hillary looked great, even though I knew from experience how exhausting this work is. She was doing three of these on some days: a brunch in the late morning, a barbecue in the afternoon, and a dinner at sunset. I started to get worried that she was pushing herself too hard, but I know she felt a huge responsibility to win this election. She had been given this chance to be the first woman president, and she was determined to keep up this incredible pace of her campaign.

While I was making the rounds at these fund-raisers, Donald Trump was speaking to a big crowd of supporters in Michigan when he decided to address the African American community. He told the crowd that the Democrats were taking the minority vote for granted in this election and that the lives of people of color had not improved much at all under Democratic rule.

"No group in America has been more harmed by Hillary Clinton's policies than African Americans," he said to the cheering crowd. "If Hillary Clinton's goal was to inflict pain on the African American community, she could not have done a better job. It's a disgrace. Tonight I'm asking for the vote of every single African American citizen in this country who wants a better future . . . Look how much African American communities have suffered under Democratic control. To those I say the following: What do you have to lose by trying something new like Trump? What do you have to lose? I say it again: What do you have to lose? You're living in poverty. Your schools are no good. You have no jobs. Fifty-eight percent of your youth is unemployed. What the hell do you have to lose?"

The nerve of this guy to call out Hillary, a woman who has worked all her life for children, for fairness in the workplace, and against discrimination, while he led a company that had allegedly prevented black people from renting apartments in its buildings, and been sued by the federal government.

Yet it was impossible to refute him with facts. While Hillary, with her packed schedule of fund-raisers, soldiered on, the campaign issued a statement that listed all the ways in which Trump had taunted Obama about his birthplace and the housing discrimination in the Trump buildings. It was a dry and stiff response to a man who was an expert in playing with the emotions of despair. No one had asked me to help the campaign craft a response that would have been more suited to the audience that I knew so well. Ignoring me felt like another blow. We were almost a month into my time as chair, and Brooklyn had not included me on any of the national campaign strategy calls. I had always included the DNC chair on mine when I managed Gore's campaign. It hurt to be cut out of those.

Thankfully I had a visit with my friend Elaine Kamarck in her home on Cape Cod, which would help soothe my soul.

For me it was hard to get a perspective on how much these three short weeks had affected me, but Elaine saw it right away. I got off the ferry in Hyannis, and the look on Elaine's face was as if I had aged ten years. We've known each other since the Carter-Mondale campaign, and we don't hide anything from each other. She took me home, poured me a glass of wine, and we sat out on her deck looking out at the sea until I felt settled enough to speak freely.

It wasn't that I didn't feel free with Elaine; it was that I didn't know how to tell the story of what was happening. What could I say? What was I not supposed to say? The fear created by the hacking had thrust me into a world that I'd never had contact with before, and I struggled to describe what that experience felt like. Around a good friend like Elaine I could express what I was feeling, but it was hard to know what I was feeling.

She didn't press me too much as we sat on the deck. I think she wanted to leave the space open for me to start when and where my thoughts led me. I started with Seth.

Only to Elaine could I say that I felt some responsibility for Seth Rich's death. I didn't bring him into the DNC, but I helped keep him there working on voting rights. With all I knew now about the Russians' hacking, I could not help but wonder if they had played some part in his unsolved murder. Besides that, racial tensions were high that summer and I worried that he was murdered for being white on the wrong side of town. Elaine expressed her doubts about that, and I heard her. The FBI said that they did not see any Russian fingerprints there, but they promised to look into the case. I didn't feel comfortable enough to ask more than that first question, but his death continued to tear me up inside.

After that came the fear for the staff. This hacking had released demons in the world. I had been harassed online by people who disagreed with something I wrote in one of my columns. Attacks on me had escalated dramatically now that I was working for a female candidate. In this campaign it was as if whatever constraints that had kept people from expressing the worst aspects of their characters had been lifted, and now they were free to take to social media to humiliate, degrade, and harass with no shame, no feeling that this is not what one does in a polite society. Were we no longer civil? Had this campaign unleashed something dire and dark within us? I feared for the country, and I feared that this was no longer a fair fight.

Elaine allowed me to pour out all these emotions, and then she flipped the script. Normally when I stay with her she has big parties, but this time she did not schedule any. Elaine said she had sensed from my voice on the phone that what I needed was to decompress. She made us a New England lobster dinner, served with more delicious wine. We put on *I Am Cait*, Caitlyn Jenner's reality television show, and laughed until our sides hurt. We had to put it on pause to recover when Jenner got all these other trans people together and decided that the best thing that they could do after they all got their nails done was go out and ride dirt bikes. What woman wants to ride dirt bikes after she gets her nails done?

I know this was silly, but it was just what I needed: to be away from it all. In the mornings Elaine would go to the barn where she had her office, and I would sit on the deck with my coffee. Cocktails were at four.

One afternoon we went to Provincetown, where I was to do the meet and greet for a Hillary fund-raiser that featured Cher, whom I've known for twenty years, and comedian Kate Clinton. I contemplated whether I should take Hillary aside and share with her my concerns about how the campaign was running and what she might improve, but I remembered that when I managed Gore's campaign, I always protected the candidate.

You do not give the candidate bad news, particularly in a public place like a fund-raiser. You want them to project confidence, to feel like a winner. Hillary and I greeted each other and talked about her grandchildren, and then I steered Elaine her way. A senior fellow at the Brookings Institution and a lecturer at Harvard's Kennedy School, Elaine is a policy wonk just like Hillary. Elaine even worked for a few years in the White House when Bill Clinton was president. It was only a few seconds before her and Hillary's heads were inclined close together, deep in a discussion about some aspect of governmental regulation. This was my gift to both of them, in a way. Hillary escaped for a moment the crushing responsibility to always be trying to get more money to do something she enjoyed.

My next stop was New York. Before I left, Elaine said she had someone she wanted me to speak with. This man, she said, was very plugged into the national security community. He had worked there for many years, and he was still connected to the deepest part of that darkness. He was a good man, she said, and he was likely to be able to make sense of some of what I had been told. Intrigued, I gave Elaine the go-ahead to call him. He agreed to speak with me.

The morning before I left after four days with Elaine, I got on the phone with the man who I referred to from then on as my Spook, but he was not as reassuring as I had hoped he would be. If anything, he was the opposite. He was less interested in the hacking and the Russians, which he seemed already to know something about, than he was concerned about my personal safety.

Where did I live? Did I live alone? What kind of security system did I have at home?

I didn't have any security system, I said. Just good locks on the doors and sturdy windows.

He said I needed to have more systems to protect myself. I needed motion-sensitive lights and a power backup system in case there was an outage so that I could be protected even if someone cut the power. He wanted me to prepare for the worst. There was a tone in this conversation that put me right back into the fearful world I had been trying to avoid with this escape to Cape Cod. He was not telling me everything he knew, but he was implying that whatever I was experiencing now was sure to get worse. He didn't want to be too explicit over the phone, he said. We agreed to meet when I got back to Washington, DC.

Knowing that I needed all of these things made me feel that I needed to also do things like this to protect the DNC. I was not just worried about myself but about the kids. Seth Rich was never very far from my mind.

Home was still a ways away, though. I'd be in Brooklyn, home for a minute, and then on my way to campaign in the battleground states of Florida and Colorado.

NINE

The Smell of a Loss

While I was in Martha's Vineyard and Cape Cod, Wiki-Leaks, and its distribution partners Guccifer 2.0 and DCLeaks, had kept busy. I don't know if Guccifer is a man or a woman or a robot, but it was releasing these private items from the Democrats in a manner that seemed very attuned to the rhythm of the United States election. Before I left for Martha's Vineyard, Guccifer released cell phone numbers and passwords from the Democratic Congressional Campaign Committee so that those candidates would not begin their campaign season undistracted. Less than a week later, documents describing voting turnout models for Florida and Pennsylvania and a few other battle-ground states appeared online, along with some private emails from Rep. Nancy Pelosi's staff.

After I left Elaine's on August 23, my destination was Brooklyn. I would finally see HQ, the high-rise epicenter of campaign power. I was eager to see it, not just because I wanted to be face-to-face with the people who had been blocking my efforts. I love the atmosphere of a campaign around Labor Day, when everyone is ramping up for Election Day. I've worked on many presidential campaigns, and one of my fondest feelings is walking into the bustle of the campaign office and hearing the phones ringing and seeing the staffers and the volunteers rushing around, people in intense conversations in the hallways, making decisions on the fly. My taxi pulled up in front of the towering brick office building at One Pierrepont Plaza and I hopped out.

Security was tight. I had to be escorted up from the lobby to the offices on the tenth floor, where I felt some of that campaign energy I craved. By contrast, on the executive floor, where Hillary's top staff worked, it was calm and antiseptic, like a hospital. It had that techno-hush, as if someone had died. I felt like I should whisper. Everybody's fingers were on their keyboards, and no one was looking at anyone else. You half-expected to see someone in a lab coat walk by.

In campaigns, it's not just about electing a candidate. It's about getting citizens more engaged in their democracy and giving them a voice. The campaign succeeds when it makes supporters feel that they hold in their own hands the power to change the country. When you have that feeling, you usually aren't too quiet about it.

When I was tiptoeing around the muffled Clinton headquarters I thought of what my friend Tony Coelho used to ask me about my campaigns. He'd always ask, "Are the kids fucking? Are they having sex? Are they having fun? If not, let's create something to get that going, or otherwise we're not going to win."

I didn't sense much fun or fucking in Brooklyn.

Look, I really respected a lot of people in that building. They were my old friends. But I could see in that visit that it was run only by analytics and data, which is only part of what you need to win an election. Robby Mook believed he understood the country by the clusters of information about voters he had gathered.

I remember saying to him, after he described this very smart way he had determined which candidate people in a particular neighborhood were likely to vote for, that he was neglecting the whole story.

"If we're not talking to new people, how are we going to register new voters?"

We were talking in his corner office with a view of Brooklyn and Manhattan, a private space that I do not think he used much. I saw him as most comfortable out at a table with the others who understood his love of data. He has a cool gaze of someone who has a determined sense of values and judges everyone by those principles. That inner cool makes someone like me who runs hot feel as though I'm bouncing off the walls when I talk. Perhaps that was something he'd agree with me on, because he was not agreeing with me about the need to spend more money to encourage the Obama coalition to vote.

Even when Clinton squeaked by in the Iowa caucuses and when she took a drubbing in New Hampshire, Robby was unwavering. He had a plan and he was sticking to it. That plan was the perfect opposition to Clinton's campaign in 2008, when she lost to Obama. She nearly ran out of money in February, but this time she was cash rich and laser-focused on gathering and controlling that money. Her campaign had been riven with divisions, public arguments, and policy disputes. Robby had a campaign tightly controlled from the top, and even when things contradicted his assumptions, he always stuck to his plan. That plan did not include giving more money to me.

For Robby, everything had a sense of a scale. I had seen a little bit of this in the Obama campaign, but he was a different kind of candidate. His candidacy lent itself to microanalysis-based targeting because the support for him, and for his message of hope, was organic. The data helped bring Obama's message to an audience of people who might be receptive to his message but did not know about him.

By contrast, Hillary was a well-known candidate, on the political scene for decades. People still had doubts about her and Trump was very effective at validating and inflaming them, which discouraged enthusiasm for this familiar face. The attitude in Brooklyn was that Hillary was such a superior candidate that she had already locked up the race. Clinton's campaign needed people to call and remind them: *Hillary needs you today to go out and talk about her plan to create jobs.* Or, *Hillary needs you today to go out and talk about how she is going to protect children and child health.* I did not see that. I heard them saying that they only needed to register five new Hillary voters in this neighborhood, and seven over here.

Why five? Why not ten? Or why not fifty?

Well, that was the precise number of people we needed in order to win a precinct.

"Well, good, but you better get five more so you can go to bed thinking that you really have a margin that will win," I told Robby and his team.

They were so precise, they made me feel as though this style of politics I had learned in my forty years was about to be put out to pasture. My world was the lost art of touching people, reaching people where they live, where they eat, where they played and where they prayed.

They did understand that I had some skills to lend to the campaign effort at headquarters, and that was to bring emotion into the room. Robby asked me to address the staff and volunteers, and I gave a speech off the cuff that was designed to remind them of the reasons we do this. How we see a better future for ourselves and for our families and we want to do everything we can, sacrifice our evenings, weekends, and holidays to bring this message to the world. Campaigns offer us a rare opportunity to live our values in our daily lives, to be patriotic and honorable in a way that few things we do allow. I could feel that I had the crowd with me as I spoke, and I hoped that I left them feeling better, more enthusiastic, and able to push harder to get Hillary into the Oval Office.

I did not leave Brooklyn feeling enthusiastic, though. They saw me only as someone who could rouse up the emotions, but they were not interested in my practical advice. My feeling was that data was a tool for engagement, but there was no substitute for that human touch. This was a message that sunk to the carpet in the antiseptic rooms in Brooklyn.

And into this hushed atmosphere, week after week, WikiLeaks dropped stolen emails, thousands at a time, with the clear purpose of distraction. Every time emails were released, the press stopped dead in its tracks to paw through them and see what they could find that would embarrass the candidate or the campaign. With the damaging information contained in the leaked emails, and the antics of the GOP nominee covered hour after hour by the cable stations, it was as if Hillary was not even campaigning. She was always reacting, rarely advancing.

I had planned my trip to Florida so that I could gather evidence about how Hillary was capturing the voters there. I have an intimate knowledge of every part of Florida, which I earned in 2000, when we spent thirty-seven days scrutinizing ballots in every county of that state trying to get a win for Al Gore. I'm fortunate that I have black skin, or the scars from those thirty-seven days would be visible at just a glance. I know the politics of Florida from the swanky streets of Miami Beach to the bodegas and barrios of Little Haiti in the western part of Orlando. That was where I was headed on this trip. We had a Senate seat up for grabs as well as several Congressional seats. There would be a lot there for me to take in so that I might understand the way things were going in the campaign. Were they active and energized by the campaign? Or had the steady stream of distractions sapped the energy there, too?

The first appointment was a telephone town hall with millennials. Many of their questions were about how to find a way to sell Hillary to their peers. They were having a hard time converting Bernie supporters to Hillary supporters. They liked Hillary in a lukewarm way, but many were still yearning for Bernie. I took as many questions about him as I did about Hillary. Then one young man asked me how he was going to talk to his family. All of his relatives were voting for Trump.

I had heard this question before. Hearing it in Florida made me realize for this election I was fast becoming a family therapist. "First, don't start an argument with them, because that will only harden them," I advised. "Here's what you have to tell them. Take a look at Donald Trump's life. I know people are enamored of him that he's a businessman and people think that he's successful, but there is nothing in his history that indicates he will help people like your family. Remind them that he has stiffed so many workers, the people who have helped him build his huge hotels and casinos. Rather than pay them, he has stiffed them. Why do they think that he would not treat the country the same way?"

I felt good after that answer. I hoped the young man on the phone felt that it was a good answer, too. I was making an attempt at talking about Trump in a way that did not entangle me or them in his crazy statements and outrageous tweets. If people would pay attention to Trump's record and his behavior instead of Hillary's, this might be a fair fight.

I also visited black radio stations, where the hosts would take calls from listeners. They were not encouraging. People on the ground in Orlando said no one was talking about Hillary on the radio, and those who wanted to support her didn't have any literature to hand out or yard signs to display. Everywhere I went when I was canvassing with volunteers people were asking for the same things. They wanted a way to show their support for Hillary, and I did see a few Trump signs here and there. Nowhere did I see any visible support for Hillary.

The only signs I saw were in the campaign headquarters. I walked down blocks and blocks of Little Haiti. I did not notice one campaign sign. Brooklyn told me that the battleground states had signs. Then they said, "Don't worry about signs." They believed signs were not as important as data. Signs are an indication that there's activity. And where there's activity, there's passion. Where there's passion, there's purpose. Yet I saw none of that in these neighborhoods that should have been for Hillary.

I had scheduled an appearance on a Haitian AM radio station program, *Morning Glory with Bishop Victor T. Curry*. These Haitian stations play gospel and speak in Creole, but they do a lot of talking and some of it is about politics. The listeners are not millions of people, but the thousands that do listen have the radio turned on for hours every day. The radio brings the community together, and it costs very little to advertise there. When the bishop asked me when the campaign was going to start a dialogue with his audience, I knew what he meant by that. When were they going to spend a few hundred dollars in advertising there, which would encourage him to urge his followers to get out and vote?

I wasn't trying to rewrite Brooklyn's strategic plan and I really wasn't interested in being the campaign manager, but it was hard to hear these complaints directly from people and not relay it back to someone. I texted Marlon Marshall, Robby's lieutenant, and the director of state campaigns and political engagement, my impressions and suggestions to make sure to convey them while they were fresh in my mind. I thought this was valuable information. We were still eight weeks out from Election Day, so there was time to correct this situation. At least the campaign should be encouraged that so many people wanted to find a way to help. Marlon dismissed my report with a condescending tone in his responses. He and Robby didn't appreciate challenges to their strategy.

I did not get the feeling that I was heard, though. Instead, I got the feeling that what I was saying was further proof that I was out of step with their vision for Hillary's victory. Perhaps they thought that because the Haitians were inclined to vote for Hillary they could assume that vote was locked in and move on to a neighborhood where the votes were more contested. This ran counter to everything I had learned in politics. You build enthusiasm among those you can depend on and make that support so powerful that it spills over into the areas surrounding the little piece of turf you can depend upon. This is how you build enthusiasm for Election Day.

After nearly three days in Florida, my next stop was the battleground of Colorado, which Bernie had won. The state highlighted the campaign's other big problem: the rift between the Bernie supporters and the Hillary supporters. Brooklyn needed to concentrate on winning the election. Healing the divisions between these factions was a problem I felt the party should solve for the campaign.

I had an early flight on August 31, so I went to my hotel in Denver and took a nap. Wellington Webb, the former mayor of Denver, picked me up at the Hyatt to take me to Aurora for a campaign event. This man was bending my ear something fierce about how the senatorial candidate, Michael Bennet, was not putting enough investment in the ground game, and how Hillary had to send more surrogates to engage the electorate or she might just lose Colorado. Did she know that? She should come here, he said. This should be on her schedule for the fall.

The next day, at an event in Denver, state party chair Rick Palacio invited all the county chairs to meet with me. Again I would be the one who would take in all their criticisms and disappointments.

It was really nice outside, and I remember enjoying the cool air. I had this wistful feeling that if I could have been in control of my life I would have stayed in Colorado for a week, enjoying the mountain air. My feeling of not wanting to leave mixed with my sense of urgency for the campaign. That mood in Brooklyn was one of self-satisfaction and inevitability. The polls were showing Hillary holding steady, between five and eight points ahead of Trump and with a clear path to 270 electoral college votes. The mood I was gathering on the ground, however, was much more restless.

The meeting with the state county party chairs was combative. One man in particular I remembered from the platform committee. Dennis Obdusky had come to Orlando looking for a fight. When he saw the process was designed to hear him out, he settled down and pitched in to find language we could all agree on. We went from being enemies to being buddies. I liked people like Dennis—disrupters working for good—because I had been one when I worked on Jesse Jackson's campaign for president in 1984.

Now, in Colorado, this man I had bonded with had been elected county chair.

Dennis was concerned that there would not be a role for the Bernie folks in the state now that Hillary was the candidate.

"Well," I said. "You're here, aren't you?"

I advised Dennis that this would not be easy. No one gives up power without a fight, but he had a good position and the Bernie folks already had won a big battle. Ninety percent of the party platform represented what Bernie believed. Take the win, I said, and build upon it.

As I got to the airport to fly back to DC on September 2, my mind returned to Donald Trump's claim that the Democrats were taking the African American vote for granted.

What I had found on the streets of Orlando seemed to support it. All the data showed that 1 percent or fewer of black folk supported Donald Trump, so that vote seemed to Brooklyn to be in the bag for Hillary. No need to spend any money to court it when the poll numbers and the data points were so overwhelmingly in Hillary's favor. I knew that to be true, but there is a difference between telling a pollster that you favor a candidate and getting yourself out the door on Election Day and going to the polls. The campaign was telling people that electing Hillary would be a historic change, but in their daily lives they did not see how it would change anything for them. I didn't see much evidence that the campaign had a story it wanted to tell these voters that would persuade them otherwise.

Colorado, too, had its own air of disappointment. The Bernie supporters who were so energized in the primary season had believed that they could change the world, fight corporate corruption, and get some relief for middle-class families. They saw Hillary as not much different from any other candidate: chasing money instead of reflecting the will of the people. They were not satisfied by the strides they had made in changing the party platform victory. They saw it as a symbolic win. And they were not that far off.

We negotiate the party platform like we're writing the Constitution, but as soon as that battle is over, the candidate faces the new realities of the campaign and does whatever he or she sees as pragmatic. The platform could be seen as a yardstick to use to measure the candidates' actions, but it never has been something they are beholden to accomplish.

What I saw was a feeling of frustration and resignation rather than the energy needed to win. I've been in campaigns long enough to know what the odor of failure smells like.

And when you catch a whiff of it, no matter what the numbers say, you should worry.

TEN

Bernie, I Found the Cancer but I Won't Kill the Patient

Before I called Bernie I lit a candle in my living room and put on some gospel music. I wanted to center myself for what I knew would be an emotional phone call. I had promised Bernie when I took the position of interim chair of the DNC that I would get to the bottom of whether or not Hillary's team had rigged the party process in her favor so that only she would win the nomination. From the moment I walked in the door of the DNC a month earlier I had my suspicions, based on the leaked emails. But who knew if some emails might have been forged? I needed to have solid proof and so did Bernie.

My long call with Gary Gensler the weekend after the convention was my road map. I followed it and began to learn what I needed to know. Debbie had not been the most active chair in fund-raising at a time when Obama had left the party in significant debt. As Hillary's campaign gained momentum, she resolved the DNC debt and put the party on a starvation diet. It had become dependent on her campaign for survival, for which she expected to wield control of its operation. Debbie was not a good manager. She hadn't been very interested in controlling the party—she let Brooklyn do as it desired so she didn't have to inform the party officers how bad the situation was. How much control Brooklyn had and for how long was still something I had been trying to uncover in the month or so that I had served as chair.

By September 7, the day I was making this call to Bernie, I had found my proof and what I had found broke my heart. I thought the party I had given so much of my life to was better than this. I asked God to order my steps so that I would not stumble in calling Bernie or in taking the actions at the DNC to correct what needed to be corrected in the party.

Right around the time of the convention the leaked emails revealed Hillary's campaign was grabbing money from the state parties for its own purposes, leaving the states with very little to support down-ballot races. A *Politico* story published on May 2, 2016, described the big fund-raising vehicle she had launched through the states the summer before, quoting a vow she had made to rebuild "the party from the ground up . . . when our state parties are strong, we win. That's what will happen."

Yet the states kept less than half of 1 percent of the $82 million they had amassed from the extravagant fund-raisers Hillary's campaign was holding, just as Gary had described to me when he and I talked in August. When the *Politico* story described this arrangement as "essentially . . . money laundering" for the Clinton campaign, Hillary's people were outraged at being accused of doing something shady. Bernie's people were angry for their own reasons, saying this was part of a calculated strategy to throw the nomination to Hillary.

I wanted to believe Hillary, who made campaign finance reform part of her platform, but I had made this pledge to Bernie and did not want to disappoint him. I kept asking the party lawyers and the DNC staff to show me the agreements that the party had made for sharing the money they raised, but there was a lot of shuffling of feet and looking the other way.

When I got back from Martha's Vineyard I at last found the document that described it all: the Joint Fund-Raising Agreement between the DNC, the Hillary Victory Fund, and Hillary for America.

The agreement—signed by Amy Dacey and Robby Mook with a copy to Marc Elias—specified that in exchange for raising money and investing in the DNC, Hillary would control the party's finances, strategy, and all the money raised. Her campaign had the right of refusal of who would be the party communications director, and it would make final decisions on all the other staff. The DNC also was required to consult with the campaign about all other staffing, budgeting, data, analytics, and mailings.

I had been wondering why it was that I couldn't write a press release without passing it by Brooklyn. Well, here was the answer.

When the party chooses the nominee, the custom is that the candidate's team starts to exercise more control over the party. If the party has an incumbent candidate, as was the case with Clinton in 1996 or Obama in 2012, this kind of arrangement is seamless because the party already is under the control of the president. When you have an open contest without an incumbent and competitive primaries, the party comes under the candidate's control only after the nominee is certain. When I was manager of Gore's campaign in 2000, we started inserting our people into the DNC in June. This victory fund agreement, however, was signed in August 2015, just four months after Hillary announced her candidacy and nearly a year before she officially had the nomination.

The other campaigns—Martin O'Malley and Bernie— also signed victory fund agreements that kicked in should they secure the nomination, not seven months before. They also did not specify as much immediate control from the campaign as the one Hillary signed with the DNC.

I had tried to search out any other evidence of internal corruption that would show that the DNC was rigging the system to throw the primary to Hillary, but I could not find any in party affairs or among the staff. I had gone department by department, investigating individual conduct for evidence of skewed decisions, and I was happy to see that I had found none. Then I found this agreement. The victory fund agreement seemed to confirm my suspicions about Brandon's role. He was there to watch the money and make sure that it was spent exactly as Brooklyn wanted. He really was the clerk.

Other than that, what I found was the normal order of political business. The party did nothing different than previous presidential cycles. During the primary season they were constantly in touch with Bernie's director of delegate operations and anything they sent to Hillary they also sent to the other candidates. A defeated candidate might argue whether or not the rules were written fairly, but they were negotiated in the open with lots of input from the members of the party long before most candidates declared their interest in running. The party did that on purpose so that there could be no influence exerted by those trying to win the nomination. Bernie's supporters did not participate in these negotiations for a simple reason: he was not a Democrat at that time.

The funding arrangement with HFA and the victory fund agreement was not illegal, but it sure looked unethical. If the fight had been fair, one campaign would not have control of the party before the voters had decided which one they wanted to lead. This was not a criminal act, but as I saw it, it compromised the party's integrity.

The sadness I felt didn't just come from the fact that I could not change what had happened. I had been careful not to interject myself into this part of the election. I worried that if I did, I might end up running the party. But seeing what had happened made me acknowledge that I could have prevented this if I had been more involved. Why were the party officers not consulted about signing this agreement? Had I been chair when it was proposed, I would have gotten the officers to weigh in on this momentous decision.

The morning before I called Bernie, I felt an overwhelming sense of guilt that I had not wanted to get my hands dirty with all of this mess, and now I was up to my neck in it. And although I wanted to get all of this out into the open to prevent it from happening again, I felt terrible that I couldn't tell anyone about this except Bernie, because of the conversation I had had with the Spook.

This was the man my friend Elaine connected me to when I was visiting her on Cape Cod, a man whom she felt would be capable of explaining some of the cyber mess to me. I met him at a hotel bar the week after I returned home to Washington—just like in the movies. He had significant experience in Russia from his time working for international organizations in the days when the old Soviet Union crumbled after the fall of the Berlin Wall. Sometimes the word "spook" is considered a racial slur but I did not see it this way with my spooky friend. As the weeks of this strange election unfolded he was like a ghost who appeared early in the morning, calling me on my home landline often as early as 4 am, to tell me what to be aware of, and often knowing what would happen in the campaign days before it occurred. This quality was spooky to me, as if he operated in a mysterious world that only a few could see. In my head, the nickname stuck.

The Spook described Russian president Vladimir Putin as a man who yearned for the old order, when the Soviet Union was as big as the United States and the two countries were well-matched adversaries. Although Russia now was smaller and weaker, it was wily and well-informed about the intricacies of American politics. Russia still could have an impact in sowing dissension inside the United States. The term the Russians had for this was "active measures."

Active measures are designed to destabilize the politics of whatever country the Russians attack. They manipulate the media, spreading propaganda and disinformation along with forgeries of official documents. These active measures create discord within communities, making people doubt their leaders and believe false narratives about what is transpiring right before their eyes. As examples, the Spook pointed to people doubting that the intelligence agencies are giving the public correct information, seeding the idea that they have an agenda of their own. These active measures also create doubt about the integrity of the elections, and get people to doubt the motives of a free press.

"They call it political warfare," the Spook said. "The tool kit is called 'active measures,' and a lot of it is not clandestine."

When he described these techniques, it was as if he was describing WikiLeaks. None of what WikiLeaks did was clandestine; it was right out in the open. The impact of its actions was to split the Democratic Party into warring factions that sought to discredit each other. Inside the five days of the Democratic convention, the threats and harassment created by the leaked emails slowed the staff work considerably. The fact that we had pulled off a harmonious convention defeated these active measures that time, but it was clear that the Russians were not done yet.

As Trump was campaigning, he spoke with admiration about Putin and cast doubt on the idea that these leaked emails came from the Russians. Trump, unwittingly or on purpose, was part of these active measures. If I told the world what I had found out about Hillary's surreptitious control of the Democratic Party, I could be seen as part of the active measures, too.

My Spook didn't know me at all, but he could see my despair for the future of the country and my uncertainty about what role I should play to protect our democracy. I didn't know if there was anything I could do, or should do, to help keep the country safe. I knew I needed to make sure that we found out everything about what the Russians were doing inside the party, because the Spook said they were certain to keep trying and to escalate as the election neared.

"Nothing they are doing is a surprise," the Spook said. "TTP: tactics, techniques, and procedures that they have used in other countries and in other elections. They are doing it in the U.S., and they are not shy about it. There is an aspect about this work that breeds some arrogance and bravado. They have targeted other countries before, but they are now aiming these tools at a great power, and they have succeeded in dividing the country even before the election. This time I think they are focused on the psychology of the voter, but I would not be surprised if the next time they will try to tamper with the vote: the voter registrations, access to voting on Election Day, and perhaps the vote itself."

I left that hotel bar with a knot in my stomach. The only thing I could hope for and pray for was that Hillary would get elected. Even if I disagreed with what her campaign had done to secure control of the party, I knew when she was in power she would stand up to the Russians. She was strong and knew the international political landscape. Putin despised her, and I bet this was one of the reasons he was working so hard to make sure she did not sit herself in the Oval Office. She was our best hope, and I wanted more than I ever had before for her to win, even if in my heart I had my doubts that she could.

In the meantime I had to keep my promise to Bernie. I was in
agony as I dialed him. Keeping this secret was against everything that I stood for, all that I valued as a woman and as a public servant.

"Hello, Senator. I've completed my review of the DNC and I
did find the cancer," I said. "But I will not kill the patient."

I discussed the fund-raising agreement that each of the
candidates had signed. Bernie was familiar with it, but he and
his staff ignored it. They had their own way of raising money
through small donations. I described how Hillary's campaign
had taken it another step.

I told Bernie I had found Hillary's Joint Fundraising
Agreement, the one that Gary Gensler had described to me
when I first took over as interim chair. I explained that the cancer was that she had exerted this control of the party long before
she became its nominee. Had I known this, I never would have
accepted the interim chair position, but here we were with only
weeks before the election.

Bernie took this stoically. He did not yell or express outrage.
Instead he asked me what I thought Hillary's chances were.
The polls were unanimous in her winning but what, he wanted
to know, was my own assessment? Why should he work hard
for Hillary if it seemed as though she would win this without
question?

I had to be frank with him. I did not trust the polls, I said.
I told him I had visited states around the country and I found
a lack of enthusiasm for her everywhere. I was concerned about
the Obama coalition and about millennials. We needed to use
the platform we had negotiated that reflected the issues that had
galvanized his voters to excite the electorate to support Hillary.

I urged Bernie to work as hard as he could to bring his supporters into the fold with Hillary, and to campaign with all

the heart and hope he could muster to ensure that Hillary got elected. He might find some of her positions too centrist, and her coziness with the financial elites distasteful, but he knew and I knew that the alternative was a person who would put the very future of the country in peril. I knew he heard me. I knew he agreed with me, but I never in my life had felt so tiny and powerless as I did making that call.

When I hung up the call to Bernie, I started to cry, not out of guilt, but out of anger. We would go forward. We had to.

ELEVEN

The Collapse

Summer was over and Hillary looked tired. I saw her sitting in an armchair at the reception before she spoke at the Cipriani Wall Street restaurant in New York on the night of Friday, September 9. We were there for the DNC's annual LGBT Leadership Council dinner. I immediately noticed her face was puffy and her skin looked pale and papery. Her eyes were glazed, and she was looking off into the distance. She wasn't chatting with anyone and she didn't seem much like the vibrant Hillary I'd seen when we were fund-raising in Provincetown and Martha's Vineyard a few weeks earlier. I pulled aside her top aide, Huma Abedin, to suggest they needed to be taking better care of our nominee.

I knew how hard Hillary had worked during the weeks she spent at Martha's Vineyard. There was no way that kind of schedule wouldn't run down a younger person, and Hillary was in her late sixties. Yet the people around her didn't seem to notice the toll this was taking on her.

I was not the only one concerned about Hillary's health. Just a few days before, I'd gotten an unsolicited email from a doctor who believed that Hillary seemed run-down. The doctor wanted me to pass along a message to Hillary that fame and glory were fleeting but the body is your foundation and requires you to take care of it. She warned that if Hillary didn't get some rest, she might be looking at worse health problems. I thanked the doctor for her concern, but I had not detected any evidence of Hillary's exhaustion myself until I saw her backstage at this fund-raiser. The atmosphere was so chaotic, I was having a hard time getting anyone to pay attention when I said to one aide and then another that Hillary did not look well. Then I thought, why was I talking to them? I could just go over and talk to Hillary.

As I walked over to her she grabbed the arms of the chair and brought herself to standing but she was wobbly on her feet, steadying herself by placing her hands on a table. She laughed at herself; however, it was not the usual big, hearty laugh that came from deep down in her diaphragm, but a top-of-the-throat laugh that turned into a rattled cough.

"How is everything going, Donna?" she asked.

"It's going well," I said. "I peeked out at the crowd in the ballroom, and they all seem really excited to see you."

"Good!" she said, and then she started to cough again.

I told her that if she was going to be in town for a day or two, I suggested that she should see an acupuncturist. Alexis Herman, who served as Secretary of Labor in Bill Clinton's Cabinet, might have a suggestion, one she had referred me to who had a magic healing touch and had broken me free of a muscle ache and cramps. As her friend, I wanted to say, I thought she really should get someone to check into that cough.

Hillary was gracious in response. She thanked me for my concern and said I should give the name of the acupuncturist to Huma Abedin. I also wanted to send her some herbal tea that I found after the GOP convention in Cleveland had made me so sick that I thought I would die from coughing. Maybe, I suggested, I could get it to her the next day. Was she planning to take a little time off? I thought that would do her some good. But Hillary was not willing to upset the schedule she was on. Just like Robby, she wanted to stick to the plan.

A short time later, I was seated in the audience at the Cipriani when she strode up to the stage with her usual strong steps. Then she said something that, had she been in better health, I don't think she would have said.

"I know there are only sixty days left to make our case—and don't get complacent, don't see the latest outrageous, offensive, inappropriate comment and think, 'Well, he's done this time.' We are living in a volatile political environment. You know, to just be grossly generalistic, you could put half of Trump's supporters into what I call the basket of deplorables. Right? The racist, sexist, homophobic, xenophobic, Islamophobic—you name it. And unfortunately, there are people like that. And he has lifted them up," she said.

When she said "basket of deplorables," I knew that no matter what she said in the rest of her remarks, this would be the comment that made it on to the evening news. Did she not understand where she was? This was a public event. It was not one of those cozy little backyard fund-raisers where I'd heard her speak freely knowing that her statements were not likely to leak outside that gathering. Here, with dozens of cameras recording her, this would get back to Donald Trump and his supporters, and it would make a lot of news.

From that night forward, Trump pounded Hillary with that remark. The press were calling it her "47 percent" moment, comparing it to the time in the 2012 campaign when a waiter at a private event recorded GOP presidential candidate Mitt Romney saying that 47 percent of people would vote for Obama no matter what because they were dependent on the government. Many thought that Romney's elitist remark was a significant factor in his loss. Sure enough, after the "deplorables" comment hit the press, the Trump campaign went into overdrive, lambasting Hillary for insulting so many hardworking and patriotic Americans who just didn't happen to believe she would make a good president. Trump himself was tweeting about it, chiding Hillary for what "a terrible thing she said about so many great Americans."

It would have been better if Hillary had not attached a percentage to her comment, but since it had gone viral, I wanted her to own it. I thought she should say in clear and strong terms that she no longer found it possible to look for sugarcoated ways to state what was happening. It was time for serious introspection and for truth speaking among the Democrats, and if her words stimulated that conversation, they had served a purpose beyond the confines of this election. Too many people—even good people—were hiding their heads in the sand, and the media were providing the sand buckets, I wrote to some of the top people in the campaign.

The next day, a Saturday, the campaign issued a statement saying that she was wrong to be so "grossly generalistic" in her remarks, but would not back down, calling her opponent's campaign one that had been built on prejudice, hateful views, and cruel voices. She made good points in this statement, which didn't even seem to make a ripple on the surface of the campaign. As Minyon wrote to me in an email, this woman could not seem to catch a break.

I was home on Sunday, September 11, and aware that Hillary was scheduled to attend a morning memorial service at Ground Zero. It was a lazy morning with good weather, and I was hoping that Hillary was getting some rest after the service.

Just a bit before 10 a.m., I got an email from Jake Tapper's Sunday show producer wanting to know what I had heard about Hillary's health. Hillary had left the memorial service after only an hour, well before it was scheduled to conclude. The email said, "She fainted and was helped into the van leaving." Next John King called and said that the network had video of this.

I knew how much this could damage Hillary. In August Trump had returned again and again to the idea that Hillary "lacks the physical and mental stamina to take on ISIS and the many adversaries that we face." It was not as if Hillary was going to be on the battlefield, but the intent of this attack was clear: to make people see Hillary as a weak woman, soft and incapable of the rigors of being president. He was enjoying this line of criticism and had begun to make it a regular part of his stump speech at his rallies. On Tuesday, September 6, he tweeted that the media had never written about Hillary's "hacking" or coughing attack. I feared what he would be able to do with this video.

CNN was airing a taped show that ended at 11 a.m. In a few minutes the network would go live, and it was likely to lead with video of Hillary's collapse. I needed an answer from the campaign immediately, and I feared I would not be able to get one in time. I started emailing everyone I could think of, all the people who were with her in New York, but got no response.

When the video aired it was heartbreaking to watch. The camera angle was from behind so I could not see her face. Her trip director Connolly Keigher was right at her side, her arm linked in Hillary's. When the door to her van opened, Hillary did not step forward to enter. She wobbled and fell backward a bit. One of her legs gave way. I gasped, thinking that had it not been for Connolly's arm linked with hers she might have hit the sidewalk. Several people rushed to her side to keep her upright, but they couldn't. I saw her foot come out of her shoe. She fell forward into the van as people scrambled to keep her upright enough to continue the story that she was just fine, just a little stumble on the curb. Despite the efforts of the staff, it looked as if Hillary had fainted.

When CNN aired the tape, the reporter said that Hillary had left the event early because she was "overheated." What? Who thought that up? They made her sound menopausal, which was unlikely in a woman at the age of sixty-seven. I emailed Brooklyn to express my opinion about what a stupid explanation that was. For a campaign that had a reputation for being closed off and sometimes less than truthful, this was a huge blunder. When reporters started calling trying to find out what was wrong after she left the memorial, the campaign had not returned their calls for an hour. When they did, they offered up this "overheated" nonsense that sounded like a lie.

I was calling Minyon and Charlie, trying to figure out what I should say. My phone was jumping. The fact that the press could not get a straight explanation out of Hillary or her staff meant they turned to the next person on their list: me. I emailed advice to the campaign: "The media is going to run with the health narrative, so do not sit idly by. Get a statement from a DOC. Let the public see her and let it go. Don't sit on this. Please."

I also offered to go on television to refute rumors she was gravely ill. I was frantic to give the correct answer to the media as soon as I knew what that answer was.

The next time we saw Hillary on television was that afternoon when cameras filmed her exiting her daughter Chelsea's apartment in Manhattan's Flatiron District. She was smiling and waving to the crowd of press that had gathered out in the street, her eyes hidden by dark glasses. She didn't look bad, but she was not giving them an answer about what had happened on that curbside at the memorial. She said some nonsense about how she was fine and wasn't it a beautiful day in New York. Then she stopped to take a selfie with a little girl who had been waiting for her, and got in the SUV to go home to Chappaqua.

Again, who decided this was the best approach? She should have thanked them for their concern and told the truth about what was happening to her body. If she had been honest, we all could have moved forward. Campaigns are exhausting, and most people would understand if a candidate was pushing too hard. By shrouding this small incident with so much mystery they made it much bigger than it had been, and they also fed the impression that Hillary was lying to us. Was this a lingering effect of the concussion she suffered in 2012, where she was out of commission for weeks and had double vision for six months and later a blood clot? Did she have brain damage? Did she have Parkinson's? The rumors were flying all over the Internet.

I was now as anxious as anyone in the country about the state of her health and the state of her campaign. She was supposed to go to California later in the week on a fund-raising tour. The reporters who were contacting me wanted to know if she was going to cancel that. I kept emailing and calling the campaign, but as the hours ticked by with no response, my mind filled in the blanks with worst-case scenarios.

By evening the campaign had worked to craft a statement from her doctor saying she had allergies that made her cough and now she had pneumonia. Did that make sense? Allergies do not cause pneumonia. When you have two explanations, my gut always senses that one of them is a lie. And who was going to believe that a grandma with pneumonia would go to her daughter's house to recover with two vulnerable little ones around? The situation had to be pretty dangerous for her to risk exposing the grandbabies. The whole story stank, and the way the campaign handled it just made matters worse.

Amid this breakdown in messaging, the press and some folks inside the Democratic Party had begun to speculate how to replace Hillary as the candidate. In a way this was a bit funny to me. When I got frustrated with Brooklyn, I'd remind them that the Democratic Party charter gave me some power they could not control: the chair of the party has the ability to replace the candidate. I had not seriously considered doing it but, after this stumbling Sunday, many others in the party were.

Donald Fowler Sr., Donnie's dad and a former chair of the DNC, was quoted in *Politico* insisting that the DNC should call the officers of the party together to develop a contingency plan immediately. He wanted us to name her replacement just in case. "Now is the time for all good political leaders to come to the aid of their party," he said.

When they called me for a comment I gave a bland response about how I was glad that Hillary was resting and was looking forward to seeing her out on the campaign trail soon. This was only hours before Brooklyn announced that Hillary was canceling her fund-raising trip to California. When I heard that, I began to think maybe Donald Fowler's advice was not so far off the mark.

The announcement that her trip to California was canceled set off another frenzy. Elaine told me that she'd been getting calls from reporters who knew she was a long-time veteran of the rules committee, asking what was the procedure to replace a candidate.

Amid this tornado, I thought not just about Hillary's health but about her anemic campaign. I thought about the muffled atmosphere at the campaign headquarters in Brooklyn, so lacking in the spirit of the fight. We were in a campaign that always seemed forced to react rather than being able to advance a positive agenda. I also recalled, so fresh in my mind, the frustrations of the people I met in Florida and in Colorado. There was so much political energy on the ground—it was just looking for someone to harness it. The whole country was in an uproar and eager to carry new leadership to victory, yet they had not embraced Hillary in the way that we had hoped. The fact of her historic candidacy, this great chance, never got any comment or built enthusiasm. Perhaps changing the candidate was a chance to win this thing, to change the playing field in a way that would send Donald Trump scrambling and unable to catch up.

Trump had done things that for a different candidate would have ended his campaign, and yet he sailed through the outrage with that smug and condescending grin on his face. He was someone who had upended the rules, thumbed his nose at the keepers of decency and standards, and made his supporters feel great while he was doing it. At last the elites were on the run, he said. They no longer held the keys to success. To believe this, his supporters had to ignore the fact that Trump was a member of the elite. He was a billionaire from an Ivy League school who slid into New York real estate with a huge loan from his father. The wild mix of him being so vulgar and contemptuous, but also covered in gold, made those who supported him identify with him. As one wit put it, he was a poor person's idea of a rich person. Acting as he did, he made it very difficult for anyone to take him down, because he seemed impervious to shame.

Hillary still held a solid lead in the polls, but the gap was closing fast. In July she had led by ten points, but by early September Trump had cut that in half. Pundits analyzing the results in different states still did not give Trump much of a chance to win. He was claiming he'd take traditionally blue states like Michigan, Pennsylvania, and Wisconsin, all of which had gone for Obama in 2012. This seemed impossible to most people, but sitting alone in my house in the late hours of the evening of September 11, I had to admit his potential victory didn't seem at all impossible to me.

My thoughts turned personal. Replacing the candidate was a bold move, but it was one that Hillary would never forgive me for.

How could I do that to her? She had been my friend for decades, and the women of the Democratic Party, the women of the whole country, had been waiting nearly a hundred years for this chance to elect a woman as president. I thought of what Madeleine Albright said at a campaign rally in February, that there was a "special place in hell for women who don't help each other." She had said that before, but it felt powerful to me that evening. If I worked to replace Hillary as the candidate, more than Hillary would scorn me. Most of my women friends would, too.

But what if we lost? What if we lost to Donald Trump? I would never be able to live with that.

As the evening wore on, I unplugged my home phone. It was ringing so much. Reporters were calling incessantly, and so were my political friends all around the country. Everyone wanted the inside story of what was going on with Hillary. I didn't have it, and even if I did I could not share it.

The next morning, Monday, September 12, I snuck into the office through a back door. Reporters were camped out on the steps of the DNC. Journalist David Shuster had reported that a meeting on the future of Hillary's candidacy was imminent, although I had not called one. When I got to my desk I found I was the most popular person in the Democratic Party.

First I heard from Joe Biden's chief of staff, asking if I had time to speak with the vice president a little later that day. Gee, I wonder what he wanted to talk to me about? I got an email from Martin O'Malley, whose campaign never really did get off the ground. Once you run, though, you get that bug. I was guessing he just wanted to let me know that he was still breathing and in very good health. I got a call from Jeff Weaver, Bernie's campaign manager, asking if I had a moment to chat with Bernie. Of course I did. I always had time for a chat with Bernie. At eleven Charlie Baker, the CEO of Hillary's campaign, arrived in my office and sat down without offering an explanation. None was necessary. With all of the rumors in the press about the party considering replacing Hillary, he had been sent down on an early train to make sure that Donna didn't do anything crazy.

"Hey Charlie," I said. "Did you come down to pick up this tea I have for Hillary? I know it would help her with her cough."

I was keeping my own counsel on this, not sharing my thoughts with Charlie because I knew what his opinion was. A few hours into the day we got our talking points from the campaign about Hillary and they were awfully weak, trying to turn her neglect of her health into a demonstration of her strength of character. She had kept a breakneck pace as secretary of state and she did the same as a candidate, trying to push through her pneumonia. Instead of owning up to the shameful way that her campaign tried to disguise her condition, the talking points praised her for being so transparent about her health, tying it to her release of her tax returns when Donald Trump had not.

This seemed like the same old same old campaign rhetoric when the country was crying out in pain.

Alone in my office after Charlie left to return to New York, I started to think of what would be the ideal ticket if I could arrange to choose one. Under the process outlined in the party charter, if the nominee died, resigned, or became disabled, the party chair would confer with Democratic leaders in Congress and the states and report to a meeting of the Democratic National Committee, which is authorized to fill the vacancy.

I spun out a dozen combinations for the ticket depending on my various considerations. I would want to keep a woman on the ticket, because it would be terrible to lose this chance to have a woman president. But then it would be even worse to lose to Donald Trump. Would I want to keep Tim Kaine on the ticket? If that was the case, then I had only one choice to make. Again and again I thought about Joe Biden. He was the strongest person to appeal to the working-class voters who seemed to embrace Trump. The ticket I liked most was Joe Biden and New Jersey senator Cory Booker. I felt certain that that combination would win the general election.

Then I thought of Hillary, and all the women in the country who were so proud of and excited about her. I could not do this to them. And I could not do this to my friend. Even if Hillary was ill and the campaign had its weaknesses, the effort to replace her would be divisive. This campaign was already torn apart by the lies and insults of Trump, the hacking and the steady drip of stolen emails released almost every week by WikiLeaks. To replace her, I'd have to work on getting party support to force her to resign her candidacy. The Bernie faction would be delighted by that, particularly if they thought Bernie would be a replacement. The section of the party—the majority—that supported Hillary would oppose that strongly, and it might further deepen divisions, allowing Trump to capture votes in the confusion.

No matter my doubts and my fears about the election and Hillary as a candidate, I could not make good on that threat to replace her. This election was no joke, and we were all in it together going forward. I would not entertain any more thoughts of replacing Hillary.

Instead, I doubled down on my commitment to do everything I could to help Hillary win.

TWELVE

I Am Not Patsey the Slave

We knew there was more coming, we just did not know when. Julian Assange, the founder of WikiLeaks, had warned that batches of documents about the Democrats would be released all the way up to Election Day. Late in August, Roger Stone, that sleazy, leering, white-haired Nixon operative who was a big supporter of Donald Trump, tweeted that soon it would be "Podesta's time in the barrel." The whole Democratic party was in an anxious crouch fearing how much chaos that might add to a crazy campaign. In those weeks after Hillary's 9/11 collapse, when she rested in Chappaqua and began to prepare for the first debate on September 26, we didn't know when the hammer would fall, but we were as ready as we could be.

Working with the cyber task force, the staff and I had developed a step-by-step contingency plan for the next email dump. As soon as the documents dropped, I would release a statement acknowledging the attack. The statement would remind the world that the DNC was the victim of a crime perpetrated by the Russians to influence the election. Trump was mocking the idea that Russians were involved, even while he urged them to release more emails. The statement would also emphasize the steps we had taken to protect the DNC since the first time the Russians broke into our system months earlier. Someone who was not really paying attention might believe that the Democrats were so incompetent that they just kept getting hacked.

The second step in our response to a new document dump was for our research department to search the documents for anything that might cause trouble, and our lawyers would review them against a database to ensure that they were not forgeries. I'd then assemble our war room of experts—including the cyber task force—on a quick conference call to determine what else we needed to do.

In the six weeks since I took over as the interim chair, I was getting a daily crash course in the world of hacking, and still I thought I needed to know more. I found out at last why it had taken so long for the FBI to let us know we had been hacked. After first becoming aware of a possible hacking when they detected computers in the DNC communicating with known Russian hacking command centers, the FBI called the DNC in September 2015 and asked for the IT department. The FBI agent was transferred to the DNC's help desk—you know, the people who answer your calls if you're having trouble logging onto the network or your mouse stopped working right. The help desk employee was a contractor hired by The MIS Department, a Chicago-based technology company.

The technician thought the FBI call—made by Special Agent Adrian Hawkins—might be a prank call, not an unusual occurrence at the DNC. Agent Hawkins said he was trying to alert the party to the presence of Russian hackers in our computer network. Think about that for a minute. If the FBI—or even someone who claimed to be the FBI—called you, wouldn't you panic, just a little? Everyone I know would have an elevated blood pressure, if not a mild heart attack, when they heard a voice from the bureau on the phone.

The contractor alerted his superior that the FBI was investigating some security breaches and had asked the DNC to look for intruders in our firewall. The technician's scan of the system didn't turn up anything, so he told the FBI and his DNC superior that he didn't have anything to report. In December, Agent Hawkins gave the technician a URL for the machine that was sending out the signal to Russia, hoping having that address would help the tech office find it inside the system.

He searched but again did not find anything. Nonetheless, the idea that something significant could be wrong in our system began to sink in. They met with Agent Hawkins in January in an FBI office in Virginia. Agent Hawkins showed them logs of Internet traffic between the DNC and the Russian entity known in hacking circles as Cozy Bear. Cozy Bear was well-known to the FBI, having hacked the State Department and the White House. Still our IT department could not find the evidence the FBI was pointing to. This went on until April, when the DNC tech department observed intruders logging onto our servers. The hacker, the DNC would later come to discover, was a different hacker popularly known as Fancy Bear. That was when Andrew brought the problem to Amy Dacey, the DNC Chief Executive Officer, who alerted Debbie. Debbie called Michael Sussmann, who recommended that the party hire Crowdstrike to help us with this problem. Seven months!

The IT guy made a mistake, and a big one. What about the FBI? Aren't these guys the world's most sophisticated investigative force? They know how to read people, right? The FBI agent had to know that he had not reached the decision maker when he got this young man on the phone. The DNC offices were only a few blocks away from FBI headquarters. The agent could have walked over and asked at the front desk to speak with the boss. I believe Miss Barbara Hurd and Miss Natalie Chung would have promptly called the party CEO, Amy Dacey. Or they could have brought our chair, Debbie Wasserman Schultz, into a secure room in Congress where they hold high-security briefings, but that seemed not to have crossed their minds. By the time Debbie finally found out about the hack, the Russians had been in the system for almost a year without anyone noticing.

How had they done it? Those in the hacking world call the method social engineering. That's when a hacker distracts a target with things that are hard for most humans to resist, like adorable videos of dogs skateboarding or pandas wrestling that most people love to click on. While you're laughing, the hackers are dropping malware into your system. They can also use voice mail if the phone system is integrated with the computer network. In the case of Cozy Bear, a voice purporting to be a female journalist left messages on DNC staffers' phones asking for information on a story. While the listener was playing the message, she was unknowingly accepting malware.

I knew about phishing—a method in which a hacker sends an email that appears to be from someone the recipient trusts with a tantalizing subject header like *You Need To Read This Cybersecurity Report*. With Hillary's campaign chair, John Podesta, it was an email that looked as though it was sent by Google demanding that he change his password. When he did change it through the link the hacker provided, they got into the system on his credentials.

In other words, we were being attacked on multiple fronts at once.

You know that feeling when there are rats in the basement? You take measures to get rid of them, but knowing they are there, or have been there, means you never feel truly at peace. As I went about my daily duties at the DNC, often my mind would drift to the image of rats. In the cyberworld the initials

RAT stand for "remote access tool," nodes where the Russian rats accessed all the information the DNC held in trust in whatever way they chose.

They weren't rats, though. They were bears. They had built dens in the walls and hibernated there for months. They hibernated well, inside big computer operating systems like Windows or popular software like Adobe Creative Suite so that a routine security sweep would not detect them. Cozy Bear and Fancy Bear were rival intelligence agencies. Putin had pitted his cyberforces against each other. Some might see this as a waste of resources, but it had made them fierce competitors who were motivated to be aggressive and take chances. They sought to undercut each other at every move, stole sources from each other, and grabbed all the goodies for themselves. Fancy Bear and Cozy Bear often went after the same target just to see who would win. One report called their cybertools ingenious in their simplicity and power.

My primary teacher in my hacking crash course was Shawn Henry, the man from CrowdStrike who was quoted in the *Washington Post* article I'd read in what seemed like a lifetime ago. Through him, I saw all of this more clearly. Even after the convention, we did not know for certain that the Bears were out of our system. In politics things have a tendency to get ratcheted up, but talking to Shawn and the cyber task force had the opposite effect. We became sober and deliberate. Shawn has that sterling military demeanor I respected in my dad, but in a bald-headed white man. He has piercing blue eyes that size up a room quickly, and you know that with that laser gaze he's very hard to fool. Yet because he is a good man, a patriot and cyberwarrior for our side, being around a man with that character has the effect of putting you at ease. With those watchful eyes on our side, you can feel safer, and that was his goal with his advice on how we should change our computer protocols.

Once I became chair we installed new security measures. Everyone on the staff was required to log off any time they stepped away from the computer, no exceptions. Logging in required two-step verification: the system would send a code to your cell phone that allowed you to log back in, so you could not do it only via your password. We no longer used the DNC email system for important communications. Any sensitive phone calls took place via FaceTime audio, and we were advised not to talk freely while standing in front of a window.

I remember the day I jotted down that advice in the sage green notebook I used for my cyberbriefings. At the top I put a gold-and-purple logo sticker from LSU, my alma mater, and at the left corner below, a midnight blue circle with white letters that said VOTE FOR SETH RICH. When I shut that cover after the conference call, I stood up from my desk to look out over the railroad tracks that first drew me to this room. *Maybe I shouldn't have my desk in front of this window*, I thought. The space from here across the tracks was open. What if there was a sniper hiding in those trees across the way? For the first time since I moved in, I closed the blinds. That was what this election was doing to us: making us doubt the things that steadied us.

I could feel another kind of hush in the office, the hush of fear, reticence, and suspicion. In September and October of an election year, the DNC is jumping, and few people usually go home before 8 or 9 p.m. This election season, I could see people watching the clock. Some of them were even leaving early. This was a different cyberhush than the one from Robby's team in Brooklyn, where the young men were focused and bonded and could work late into the night with fingers fast across the keyboards. At the DNC we looked at our computers warily, not knowing if they could be trusted.

When I looked around the office at night, the only person I saw was often Adam Parkhomenko, the DNC field director. I eventually asked him to move his office to the empty one near mine so that I could feel safer staying late. Adam was also a reserve police officer, and I was grateful to have him there, but I wanted more energy in these rooms. The lack of enthusiasm I saw as I traveled the country was something I couldn't stop on my own, but I was not going to let it linger at the DNC if there was something I could do about it.

To help boost morale, I decided I'd hold impromptu parties in Debbie's office. I called it my Wings and Wine Caucus. I have always loved wings and I believe they pair well with wine, but I'd offer beer, too. Debbie left behind some pretty good wine, and by the time we got through that, people were starting to stay later and work better together.

At first Wings and Wine was a big confessional. I heard how the hacking was affecting the staff in their lives outside the office. Tom McMahon said he kept finding himself in places where the people around him were speaking Russian. He did not recall that had ever happened before. My assistant, Anne Friedman, was very conscious of her phone. She had been sitting out with friends on the deck enjoying a summer evening when she started to wonder if the Russians had turned on the microphone in it. Both Tom and Anne tried to talk themselves out of this paranoia. That was ridiculous, they agreed, and called it lunacy. But was it? As I looked around the table, I wondered how many others had had moments, like I'd had at my office window, when they second-guessed their safety. This is what the Russians were doing to us, too.

These meetings were helpful in other ways. We bonded with each other, even bonded through those fears. Everyone was invited, but you know how that goes. After a few times you are down to a core group with a few surprise guests every once in a while. I already knew Tom and Anne, the daughter of a close friend, but I got to know Julie Greene, Patrice Taylor, and Adam Parkhomenko better. Also, I learned to trust Charles Olivier, the CFO sent down by Brooklyn, and he grew to trust and later to respect me.

I was suspicious of Charles from the beginning, because he was good friends with Brandon. Now that he was a regular part of Wings and Wine, the barriers between us were starting to fall, and he was open to my questions about how I was perceived in Brooklyn. It was still chapping my hide that they did not include me on the national election strategy conference calls, as if my decades of experience in the black community were not needed for a victory in November.

Over many evenings of Wings and Wine, I got Charles to describe the point of view Brooklyn had of my old, ragged ass. To Robby's boys, my moment of glory had been the Gore campaign, which we lost. To them my campaign knowledge was from a bygone era. The common wisdom was that my inability to accept that things were different now was what was making me so feisty (meaning "unpleasant to work with"), but the truth was that no matter how much noise I made, my thoughts were irrelevant to them. I saw myself as making a sacrifice to help the party. They saw me as desperate for significance and trying to claw my way back into the national conversation.

This was so off the mark it made me laugh, and it was also very useful information. They didn't want to hear from me, and obviously it would make them happy if I would just go away. *Okay, boys*, I mused, *give me a lump sum to spend on rousing up people of color and I'll leave you and your data points alone. You ain't gonna get this on the cheap, though.*

After the session with Charles, when I came to understand my relationship to Brooklyn, I looked over the list I'd made at the Broadmoor Hotel when I was in Colorado Springs. It was nine pages of detailed cost estimates for advertising buys and literature in communities of color in almost every state, but particularly in the battleground ones. I was still trying to get that $8 million. In a campaign that was well on its way to raising a billion, that was a pittance.

I called Brandon and Charles into my office to talk about getting this money out of Brooklyn. Automatically Brandon was a no, absolutely. I was not asking for his permission. I was asking for his tactical advice in getting what I wanted from Brooklyn. His best friend was Heather Stone, the chief of staff in Brooklyn. She could shut this down if she chose. Brandon was the one choosing, though. Oh, no, he said. You are not going to get $8 million. They are not going to give that much to you to manage. You should ask for $2 million.

This was not a consultation as far as I was concerned, and I was not finding his advice to be useful. When he said I wouldn't get $8 million I thought he was operating as my emissary in the negotiations. I had offered to take it down to $7 million and then $6 million, ready to settle this and get to work. Then a day later he told me it was all set. They're transferring $2 million.

"As an initial payment?" I asked.

No, he said. That was it. That was all that I would get.

Said who? Had Brandon even submitted my numbers to Brooklyn? This was not a miscommunication. He said he got what he could get, but I don't think he even tried. I sensed that he and Heather had agreed on $2 million, and he'd just waited a while to let me think there was a negotiation. Then Charles came in to ask if we knew why Brooklyn had just transferred $2 million into our accounts.

They transferred the money so fast it was as if they were showing me the window was closed. Not a chance to ask for more. What gave Brandon the right to decide this? I was furious, and he seemed almost amused at my rage.

That night at Wings and Wine I had more wine than wings. I was taking a second look at Charles. Was he really here for me? Or was he Brandon Number Two?

I told Charles that I wanted to talk to him. How was he moving between these two parts of the campaign? Who did he think he answered to? He had the perfect answer. He was going to have conversations with Brandon, but he never wanted me to think he didn't have my best interests at heart. He would be honest with Brooklyn, but the person he reported to was me and he understood his fiduciary responsibility was to the DNC.

"Okay, Charles," I said. "Let's figure out how I can raise $6 million."

Wings and Wine was fun that night. Everyone had come to the DNC from different constituencies. Some of the staff were from nonprofits, some from unions, and others from businesses. All of them remained connected to their former jobs. We decided to meet again the next day with lists of organizations that had not reached their limit in campaign or political contributions. The next day we had a pretty good list of places we could ask to contribute to the DNC, and I asked everyone to start making calls, and I made some calls on my own. The campaign to raise money for our Victory Fund went great the first day, with strong responses, and lots of pledges to contribute. By the next day someone had leaked that list to Brooklyn. When I started to make my calls that afternoon, I found that Brooklyn had gotten there first and captured that money. Now they wouldn't even let me raise my own money.

I know Charles was working his best for me, even if he was a double agent. He kept telling Brooklyn I was not going to let this go. I had heard that Brooklyn planned to put me on the road as a top surrogate just to get me out of the building. I wished I could tell them that was a bad idea, because what I saw in the battleground states only increased my sense of urgency.

I asked to get Charlie Baker, Marlon Marshall, and Dennis Cheng from Brooklyn on a conference call so that we could straighten this out. This was not a pleasant conversation. My emotions were high. I felt like I wanted to set the record straight. I gave up everything for this miserable job! I also knew that the woe-is-me tactic was not going to get me any respect or any money so I dropped that, but the wound still ached. Why were they making it so hard for me to do my job? I was not getting anywhere with them, though. They were holding firm on the $2 million, and also on the idea that they needed to control every dollar raised from now until November.

"All I want you to do is to treat me with some respect," I said, my voice rising. "I'm not Debbie, I'm not Hannah, and I'm not Patsey the slave."

There was no response to that name. I didn't believe that these nice liberals would have missed seeing the film *12 Years a Slave*, in which Solomon Northup's friend Patsey was played so well by Lupita Nyong'o, who won the Oscar for the role.

"Patsey the slave!" I said. "Y'all keep whipping me and whipping me and you never give me any money or any way to do my damn job. I am not going to be your whipping girl! From this time on, we're keeping the money we raise, is that clear? Patsey is keeping her money!"

I could only imagine their faces when I dropped that line. Calling them out that way was crude, but it was effective. Finally they allowed me to raise my money to fund the DNC's outreach to the minority community using Michelle and Barack Obama in our advertisements and some targeted funds for the state campaigns.

I got daily reports from Andrew Brown, our CTO, and often the news was that the Russians were attacking the system, trying different routes to get in. I put a big calendar on my office wall and placed a yellow or green X on the days when the Russians were active. It was breaking my heart that this attack on our democracy was not getting more attention from everyone in DC. I was using my connections to the Democratic powers that be to get them to talk about it. The media was still covering it like these were "alleged" attacks, unproven. Why wasn't Obama saying something? Where were the intelligence agencies? This was a national emergency.

On September 22 Congressman Adam Schiff, ranking member of the House Intelligence Committee, and Senator Dianne Feinstein, vice chair of the Senate Intelligence Committee, made a first step. They issued a statement about the hacking, saying it had taken place on direct orders from Vladimir Putin, who was "making a serious and concerted effort to influence the election." They called on him to halt. "Americans will not stand for any foreign government trying to influence our election. We hope all Americans will stand together and reject the Russian effort."

I wasn't clear on what that statement was supposed to make people do. How do Americans "stand together and reject the Russian effort"? Do we shake our fists at Vladimir Putin from across the sea? It was another drop in the ocean of confusion created by Donald Trump. In the preparations for the first presidential debate, it hardly got noticed.

The first presidential debate was at Hofstra University in Hempstead, Long Island, set for Monday, September 26. I had never seen a rumble of anticipation like the run-up to this debate. It was like Donald Trump was back in WWE wrestling. The networks hyped this contest endlessly, with journalists denigrating Donald's ability to outmaneuver Hillary because she was such a practiced debater. The rumor was that Donald had refused to do debate prep. He was so confident that he'd do well that he didn't need any coaching. This set the tongues a-wagging, because everyone knew how thoroughly Hillary prepared for everything. This would be a clash of styles and temperament for the whole country to judge.

There was also the question of Hillary's health, which was a subject of endless speculation. One *New York Times* reporter wrote, "Her dismal public standing on questions of candor, combined with decades of conspiracy theories about her health, had already produced an uncommon challenge for aides and supporters seeking to tamp down speculation about her physical condition." You'd think she was going to stumble onto the stage and collapse, but the press was always ready to pounce on Hillary, who by the day of the first debate was only two points ahead of Donald in the polls.

That morning I booked myself on as many talk shows as I could to spread the word about the virtues of Hillary and how she was a formidable opponent. I wanted to have some war paint on—makeup that would not just make me pretty but let the world know that I was prepared to kick some ass. GMA anchor Robin Roberts hooked me up with her makeup artist, Elena George, a great gift from one tomboy to another. At one of the early primary candidate debates, Elena had put these mink eyelashes on me. From that moment I looked better and felt stronger. I knew if I had those mink eyelashes I could do anything.

I felt I looked good in my tan jacket and black skirt with those heels that you only wear twice a year, like Easter shoes. I had lost weight on the stress diet of salad and wings and scotch. My exercise regimen was running through airports, so I felt fit, as I had been doing a lot of that.

My message about Hillary on these morning shows was that this was her moment to pivot, to talk about the future she sees for the country and take the world's focus off the past. I knew that I would also face questions about her health. Donald kept talking about stamina but it was code for her being a woman, being weaker and a bit confused by the big old complex world around her. This insult was not lost on women, and we talked about her resilience. As we got to Hofstra University for the debate, I knew this was not David vs. Goliath, but it had that kind of mood.

I was honored that the campaign seated me in the front, next to Vernon Jordan and Bill Clinton, those two old dogs. This is one of those moments when a lady keeps her knees together. I was sitting in high cotton. Chelsea Clinton was sitting on the other side of her father. Terry McAuliffe and many other prominent Democrats were seated in the row behind me. The auditorium was buzzing with excitement as the moderator, Lester Holt, took his place at the desk facing the stage, with the audience craning their heads around to see who else was in the room.

Trump walked across the stage like he was a gangster, like the village thug straight out of Queens. There was so much sexism around Hillary I was praying that she looked good that night. When she walked onto the stage I thought, *Praise the Lord, she looks fantastic*. She looked rested and refreshed, bright and shiny, the best of the best. He looked not like he came to debate but to beat her up.

This was the wrong arena for him to win that. Women of Hillary's era, like Eleanor Holmes Norton, are thinkers. They are brainiacs. They have shattered so many glass ceilings that they just dust those shards off their shoulders and keep on. That night Hillary came to represent.

Sitting there in the front row, I kept thinking to myself that Donald was not prepared for this. I could hear him sighing. Al Gore got into so much trouble in one of our debates because people thought his sighing was condescending. With Donald it was more of a snort and a sigh, snorffling. He was so insecure on that stage, he had to keep interrupting Hillary as she spoke, which made him look weak, as if he was scrambling. It was clear to me that he didn't really know why he was running for president. On the other hand he knew exactly what he was doing, even though he did not come to the debate well rehearsed. These guys had it all sewn up in the bag. They didn't spend much money campaigning. I guess he felt he didn't need to prepare because he knew the Russians were taking care of this for him.

Hillary scored many points on him that night, but there were two that stuck out for me. One was when she mentioned that the Russians were hacking our election and he disputed it. He said it could be China, or it could be a four-hundred-pound guy sitting in his bedroom. Wow! I felt certain he was going to live to regret that statement. I just didn't know how impervious he was to regret.

The other thing that made me smile was when he went after Hillary for her stamina, noting she had been off the campaign trail for weeks, implying she was so frail she needed two weeks to recover from her fainting episode. She was ready for him. She said, yes, she had been away preparing for the debate. And then she added with a big smile, "preparing to be president."

I was sure every woman who has been marginalized and ignored by a male boss who seems to have no skills other than his authority over her recognized the expression of triumph on Hillary's face.

In the spin room after the debate, all the Hillary surrogates felt her victory. She was back. This was not the Hillary who had stumbled two weeks before. This was the Hillary we all believed in. She made us proud, she looked good, and everything worked as we hoped it would. I was proud of her posture, her demeanor, her stamina, and her ability to connect with the audience.

Across the room, Trump was blustering and making excuses. "They . . . gave me a defective mic! Did you notice that?" As the interview went on, he hammered his point. "I wonder. Was that on purpose? But I had a mic that wasn't working properly."

I really did see the pivot in Hillary's performance that I had hoped for, and I was confident at that moment that the campaign could use the energy from this to get back on target.

I was doing my own little tweet storm that night praising Hillary:

"Trump wanted to talk about 'stamina,' but he ended up looking like Babe Ruth trying to run a marathon."

"Hillary's suit was bright red . . . and by the end of the night, so was Trump's face."

And the best one at 11:30 p.m.:

"Hillary Clinton's strong performance shows she is the only candidate READY and qualified to serve as president."

Yes, and for the first time in a while, I believed she would be.

THIRTEEN

Hacker House

Every week when I dialed into the conference call with the cybersecurity task force I had recruited to prevent the DNC from being hacked again, I learned more about the hacking. I came in thinking I knew more than the average person might about the world of the Internet. Hell, I'd run a presidential campaign for the guy who invented it. What I found out on these weekly phone calls was that I didn't know nothing.

One of the task force members was Aneesh Chopra, who had been the nation's chief technology officer. Aneesh had been working with government policy on technology for his whole career, and his calm and steady voice and simple language when he taught things I needed to learn was respectful and coherent. I recognized that he had had to explain complicated things like hacking to many government officials over the decades, and he had perfected a method of communicating with us. Like most of the nation and like most who had served in the government, when I pictured hackers I thought of disgruntled loners, or computer guys who just wanted to see if they could break into a company or a government. You know: the aforementioned four-hundred-pound guy sitting on his bed in his underwear.

Aneesh explained my idea of these hackers was stuck in the 1990s. Back then hackers had been pranksters, or solo operators with a grievance, like an environmentalist who hacks into a logging company website to disrupt their operations, or someone who had a beef with an ecommerce site who takes it down for a day or two, costing the company thousands of dollars of revenue. That was then. Now I needed to think of the hackers who had attacked the DNC as soldiers who wore crisply pressed military uniforms and clocked in to work precisely on time, dedicated to their mission to disrupt politics any place their government chose as a target. The four-hundred-pound hacker might noodle around trying to break in and be excited if he got lucky. If he didn't, he'd move on after a few hours. Our hackers worked this as a full-time job and they were relentless.

In the last fifteen years, hacking had become a government operation done by well-trained teams. For a very small investment on the part of the government they served, these dedicated teams of hackers would break into big companies to steal intellectual property like proprietary methods of rolling out steel or design schematics. Big corporations like Goldman Sachs or Walmart knew this. They are being attacked all the time and, because of that, they build cybersecurity into their budgets. For them it is a cost of doing business.

Governments have not been doing the same, and they have not built very strong barriers to hacking. The government's notion of a cyberthreat was mostly limited to an enemy trying to disrupt our power grid or our water system. The government's low-cost calculation was that if they kept the computers that run the electric grid or the reservoir pumping station disconnected from the Internet, they wouldn't have to worry too much about being hacked. In the last eight years the government has started to spend a lot more money on cyber protection but one could argue that they need to spend it smarter because, as we saw at the DNC, the threat is increasing.

Hacking expanded into geopolitics early in this century when governments started hacking their political adversaries. The Chinese hacked the 2008 U.S. election, breaking into the Obama campaign to collect political information about the candidates and opposition research. While the method was unexpected, what they gathered from the intrusion was the kind of information that any government would want to know about who might be running the United States after the next election. The Obama hack was an act of espionage, but it was not a big blow to the operation of the party or of the election.

At first the DNC had assumed that when Cozy Bear and Fancy Bear gained entry to the DNC's servers, they were after the same kind of material the Chinese had sought in 2008. Although the Russians had sown disinformation through fake news in the Ukrainian election in 2014 and hacked into the election system to manipulate the vote totals, no one thought they would be bold enough to try something like that in the United States. Nor did anyone suspect that they had the political sophistication to weaponize the information they had gathered from our servers, understanding exactly when they should release which emails they had stolen, so that the information would have the maximum impact on the voting population. Our hacking was unlike anything members of our expert task force had ever seen. This was one of the reasons why the DNC didn't respond as aggressively as it might have when the officers found out it had been hacked. What happened to us had no precedent in American politics.

Although these cybersecurity task force calls were all about solving the problems ahead and not looking back to assign blame, I could hear the incredulity in the voices of these experts. They were appalled by how easy it was to break into the DNC. One member used the warm-knife-through-butter analogy. Another described the network as "wide open," and all of them were alarmed that the party did not have an employee whose sole job it was to protect our information. I remember one task force member comparing the DNC to a small business whose only asset was information, and yet we had no resources devoted to protecting the one thing of value that we had.

If the DNC was a small business, it was like no small business I've ever seen. We change bosses and objectives with each election cycle and our goal is to spend every dime we raise to get people elected. Long-term planning for things like investment in cybersecurity is hard to do in this environment. And in this cycle it sometimes seemed like Brooklyn wanted to strip it of its functionality nearly as much as the Russians had.

We had a few information technology people in the building who were employees of the IT firm we contracted, but we did not have a chief information security officer, or CISO, a job title I'd never heard of before. This is a person whose whole job it is to keep your data safe. Instead we had The MIS Department, that Chicago-based IT firm that we'd inherited from the Obama campaign. Despite the fact that Obama's 2008 campaign had been hacked, the company had become the IT contractor for Democratic party operations all around the country, including the DNC. If we'd had a CISO who was savvy in the ways of Washington, DC, when the FBI called to say we had been hacked by the Russians, that person would have run to the chair's office with hair on fire.

Another person on those calls who was educating me was Michael Sussmann, the former cybercrimes prosecutor for the Justice Department. He was the one who recommended Shawn Henry and CrowdStrike. As an executive assistant director at the FBI, Henry had overseen cybercrime investigations all around the world. He had been working there when the Chinese hacked the Obama campaign. The DNC had hired CrowdStrike in May to help us get a handle on our hacking.

These two men were more than that to me, though. When you enter this world of cybercrime, suddenly everything you touch and see seems not to be what you thought it was. Are people listening to you? Are you safe in your car driving down the street? If I called Shawn or Michael, they would answer my anxiety with steady voices. They would explain the situation carefully and, whenever I spoke to either of them, I would come away thinking we had a handle on this. Caution was necessary, but panic and paranoia were a choice, and one I could not make because it would cloud my thinking. We might not have this thing solved, they would assure me, but we were making progress.

Initially the progress came from the program called Falcon that CrowdStrike placed on the DNC servers. I imagined our Falcon watching the activity in the system like a predator, looking for anyone who started to meddle. Falcon was like a window into the system with a video camera that recorded everything that went on inside. Through it, we were able to see Russian actors who were logging on to the system and how they were talking to the computers inside our network. The CrowdStrike analysts showed us how the Russians were reaching out from thousands of miles away to control our system. They had installed software that could send the information they were interested in back to their own servers and issue commands for the malware to take specific actions. As soon as CrowdStrike installed Falcon, it detected an intrusion underway with two Russian state actors digging deeper and deeper into the DNC.

In May, when CrowdStrike recommended that we take down our system and rebuild it, the DNC told them to wait a month, because the state primaries for the presidential election were still underway, and the party and the staff needed to be at their computers to manage these efforts. For a whole month, CrowdStrike watched Cozy Bear and Fancy Bear operating. Cozy Bear was the hacking force that had been in the DNC system for nearly a year. That Bear was clever, using a number of maneuvers so that it remained undetected. Cozy Bear would have been happy to stay inside our system for as long as possible, quietly vacuuming up information as the campaign continued to the general election. Fancy Bear showed up in April 2016. Fancy Bear, the one our IT department detected, was loud and did not seem concerned about being found out. As our technology director Andrew Brown said, it was like Fancy Bear smashed in the front window and raged around grabbing whatever was at hand, less concerned about being detected than Cozy Bear had been.

My task force was appalled at the idea that CrowdStrike had to wait a full month before they took down and rebuilt the system because this was not what a business would do. I also had sympathy for the choices made amid the chaos of the primary season. After CrowdStrike rebuilt the system, all of our staff had to learn new computers, new log-ins, new procedures, at the moment when their personal lives were being destroyed by these leaks. Then their bosses resigned because of the emails that were distributed by WikiLeaks, creating even more chaos and insecurity. All of this was on top of a contentious campaign. Our regular task force conference calls gave me a new appreciation of the dedication of our staff, who endured this incredibly stressful time.

The purpose of these weekly calls was not to look backward, though, but to look forward to what we needed to do to survive the election and beyond.

The task force felt good about what the DNC and CrowdStrike had done to kick the Russians out of the system in the six weeks after Falcon was deployed. Falcon also put up some barriers against the Russians returning, but no barrier they could erect was fail-safe. Part of what Falcon offered us was forensics. The program burrowed into the activities that had taken place in the last few years to uncover Cozy Bear's goals, but we still were not sure that we knew everything that it had accomplished. One of the task force members compared it to coming home to find out that the front door was broken open. You walk through the house trying to find out what was stolen. Did the intruder eat from the fridge? Use the bathroom? Rifle through your drawers? We didn't know the extent of what they had taken. They are very good at covering their tracks.

Call by call, as the task force analyzed every detail of the DNC hack and response, the consensus was that we needed to buy a robust cyberdefense software program and to contract a team that could make these defenses even stronger and train the staff to respond quickly to incidents as they were uncovered. Ideally this team could stay with us up until the election. The problem, as always, was money.

By the beginning of September our cyberdefense already had cost us $300,000, and the bills were still coming in. When then FBI Director James Comey testified before Congress in January 2017 about our hacking, he said that the DNC had denied the FBI access to our servers when they wanted to investigate. I was not sure what he was talking about. Maybe he was referring to that period of time before we took the hacking seriously, when the IT department believed that the calls from the FBI were a prank. We never handed over the physical servers, though, because the FBI never requested them once we were working together. If you unplug the server to bring it to the FBI, disconnecting it erases part of the server's memory. What was much more useful to the FBI was for us to create an exact copy of the contents of the relevant servers, laptops and other devices. This was much like when the police investigate a robbery. They don't need to take the surveillance cameras back to the office with them; they need what was recorded on them. The FBI sent us an itemized list of the things they wanted us to provide for their investigation and Crowdstrike helped us check off every item on that list.

Making those clones so that the FBI could conduct a thorough investigation was expensive. The software we needed was expensive, too. Even more expensive was the suggestion to bring on what they call an incident response team. These are the computer whizzes employed by every big company. They are the ones who respond when an outsider breaks into the system. They have decades of experience blocking these intruders, and that kind of knowledge does not come cheap.

Late in August Nicole Wong, a member of our cybersecurity task force, had a great idea. Why didn't the DNC recruit volunteers?

When she first suggested this I thought it would never happen. I mean, these antihackers are much in demand, make huge salaries, and likely were not at all interested in politics. Maybe I was betraying my bias here, but I could not imagine a world in which these top professionals would want to leave the comfort of their California homes and come to DC to live in some rented house so that they could help out the DNC. Why would people want to invite that stress into their lives?

Nicole knows this world better than almost anyone, having served as a deputy U.S. technology officer in the Obama administration and also as a vice president and deputy counsel at Google and the legal director for products at Twitter. She assured me that my bias was just that. What would appeal to them, she said, is that this was a hard problem, just the kind of thing that they enjoy. She assured me that they liked few things better than being dropped into the middle of a high-stakes crisis. This is when they feel the most alive and on their game. The aspect of our problem that would attract them was that they would be going after the Russians, an adversary few of them had faced before. Plus, Nicole said, the limited nature of the job— only until the election—was something else they'd like. They could come in, do their best, and go home knowing they had done something great for the country.

Well, all right then, Nicole. A big part of me still did not believe her. I mean, living in this fearful atmosphere every day since I became interim chair made me think that no one in their right mind would say *hell yeah* to this mess. As with all things cyber, my instincts were off by a wide margin. Nicole knew all the people we needed to tap on the shoulder. Her first calls were to three senior-level engineers who, in turn, reached out to their friends and got recommendations for others whom Nicole might want to talk to about this opportunity.

One of her first calls was to Heather Adkins, with whom she had worked at Google. Nicole described Heather as "the best of the best," someone everyone talked reverently about. Heather kept a low profile but was well-known in the world of cybersecurity. Nicole also called Ryan McGeehan, who led the incident response team for Facebook for many years and has a great reputation in the industry. When I heard he was from Facebook I was impressed. Imagine how many different evil forces, domestic and international, are trying to wiggle their way into Facebook every minute of the day, as well as the scams and the fake identities he would have to deal with in that job. Our little DNC hack was nothing compared to that, except for the global consequences.

Ryan, in turn, recommended Rob Witoff, who was in charge of infrastructure and security at Coinbase, the largest cryptocurrency firm in the world and who had previously worked at Jet Propulsion Laboratory on lasers for the International Space Station. Robb was well known for his skills as an engineer as well as his effectiveness at leading teams.

All of these top professionals she called were excited about the assignment. "It just goes to show how passionate people were about protecting the vote," Heather said. I couldn't argue with that! Nicole said she was looking for two things in members of this team: engineers who were the best in the business and also knew how to get along as a team.

The assignment was short—at most a month but she thought it might be much shorter—and any ego clashes or individuals who were using this as a way to advance their careers might slow progress. By the end of September Ryan and Rob agreed to relocate to DC for the first two weeks of October.

Heather and Nicole flew to DC on September 26 to assess the situation so that they could describe it to the volunteers before they arrived. What they found was a system they saw as functional, but not very well maintained. The analogy Heather used was driving an old car from the 1970s. "It's barely running and you keep duct-taping it together," she said. "It will get you from point A to point B, but it does not have many safety mechanisms." Still, the situation was familiar to them. As Nicole said, "It was not something we hadn't seen before."

Perhaps this was why Rob thought that he would be in DC only for a week or two. "Everyone I spoke to said that things were not that bad," Rob recalled. "They just needed a little help to make sure that things did not get worse." He and his girlfriend had planned a trip to Paris for the end of October. His assumption was he'd spend a few weeks helping the DNC get its system ready for Election Day, and then he'd meet up with his girlfriend in France.

Ryan McGeehan and Rob arrived in DC on the same day and the next morning made their way to the DNC to take a look at our system. The computer space at the DNC is a thin room on the first floor that wraps around the side of the building. Rob and

Ryan arrived there on October 5, only five days after they'd spoken with Nicole, carrying brand-new laptops they bought especially for this task. These machines had never been connected to the Internet before they arrived with them in DC, and Rob and Ryan used fresh email addresses and user names because they assumed that any computers connected to the DNC network would be compromised. That morning they met first with Andrew Brown, our CTO, to discuss the challenges they needed to address, and then Andrew took them into the belly of the cyberbeast.

Andrew, Ryan, and Rob had just stepped foot into the computer room when someone popped up from his cubicle.

"Guys, I think we have a problem here," the technician said. "I just got a call from MIS and they say we're under attack."

"This is a pretty shitty welcoming gift," said Ryan. He opened up his laptop and signed into the system. Rob pulled over a whiteboard and started to work on the incident timeline. They had been in the DNC less than a minute and they were already in the middle of our crisis.

FOURTEEN

October Surprise

We were one month away from the election and I was worried about an October Surprise. Campaigns are always jittery in October. They suspect their opponents have saved something to leak to the press that will disrupt the campaign without leaving enough time to recover. Often these fears prove to be unfounded. But after the surreal campaign of 2016, an October Surprise felt almost inevitable.

Lauren Dillon, the research director of the DNC, thought the surprise would come from WikiLeaks. She was in charge of monitoring the WikiLeaks dumps and analyzing their contents. Whoever at WikiLeaks was deciding what to drop and when had a sophisticated understanding of American politics. The emails they dumped right before the Democratic convention were cherry-picked to create the maximum disruption inside the Democratic Party. As October opened, Lauren cautioned that something bigger than all that had come before was likely to hit us soon, and I tried not to imagine what that could be. My experiences with October Surprises seemed irrelevant to a campaign that suffered three or four surprises each day.

I couldn't spend much time thinking about what might come, because in the front of my mind was the hacking and Brandon. I was making progress on both. Hacker House was up and running. And Brandon was out of my hair! As the month of September drew to a close, the tension between Brandon and me had gone from subtle to visible. When I described my goals and strategies at staff meetings, Brandon often rolled his eyes as if I was the stupidest woman he'd ever had to endure on his climb to the top. He openly scoffed at me, snorting sometimes when I made an observation. He and his buddy Doug Thornell sat together at the end of the table exchanging knowing looks whenever I opened my mouth. I bet they talked about me often. I wondered what my nickname was. This condescension infuriated my assistant, Anne, who saw this behavior as outright sexism, but I didn't have time for that. I just wanted him to go away. Every time I saw him in the office my stomach flipped. I sent an email to Brooklyn saying that I was done with him. I wanted him out of the DNC but Brooklyn objected to firing him. Then suddenly God sent me a miracle: the Forward Together Bus Tour.

Someone in Brooklyn, maybe Brandon, came up with the idea of getting two big buses and painting them bright blue with FORWARD TOGETHER and slogans about voting and registering to vote on their sides. Brandon took charge of this effort. One bus would start in St. Louis, then circle the Midwest before heading west toward California. The other would head east and south from Ohio, focusing on the Rust Belt, Mid-Atlantic, and South. Brandon was working nonstop on the locations for the visits and arranging for local celebrities and politicians to meet them at the stops. I told Brandon I thought this was a great idea and that he should really devote a lot of time to making sure that it was a success. He was too busy going FORWARD TOGETHER to get all up in my business. Plus he seemed to be enjoying making this contribution to the campaign, so it was good for all.

After I taught my class at Georgetown October 5, I flew to Boston the next day for an event and a little fun with Mary Matalin at a forum on women and politics at Boston College. The next morning Ray Buckley picked me up at 9 a.m. for a full day in New Hampshire that would include some time that afternoon campaigning with Bernie and Maggie Hassan, who was running for Senate. I was looking forward to seeing both of them.

On October 7, after a busy morning and lunch, Ray and I drove to Nashua. My phone started rattling in my bag and I grabbed it to see what the ruckus was. I was thinking it might be something about Hurricane Matthew, the fifth named storm the nation had suffered that year. Matthew was a category five and starting to build in strength, but that was not the thing that was blowing up my phone.

The Department of Homeland Security (DHS) had released a statement about our hacking, the first sentence of which nearly brought tears of relief to my eyes: "The US Intelligence Community (USIC) is confident that the Russian Government directed the recent compromises of e-mails from US persons and institutions, including from US political organizations."

I read that sentence out loud to Ray, and he hooted. And the second sentence in the statement was even stronger:

"The recent disclosures of alleged hacked e-mails on sites like DCLeaks.com and WikiLeaks and by the Guccifer 2.0 online persona are consistent with the methods and motivations of Russian-directed efforts. These thefts and disclosures are intended to interfere with the US election process. Such activity is not new to Moscow—the Russians have used similar tactics and techniques across Europe and Eurasia, for example, to influence public opinion there. We believe, based on the scope and sensitivity of these efforts, that only Russia's senior-most officials could have authorized these activities."

Hallelujah! That's right, my fellow Americans. Putin is screwing with the election, and the *only* candidate benefitting from this is Donald Trump. Now what we had said about the hacking was backed by all the United States intelligence agencies except the FBI. Even though the FBI was not willing to sign this statement, Ray and I already knew what they had on Fancy Bear and Cozy Bear. People don't understand how hard it is for those agencies to say that they are "confident" about anything, because they are so cautious in everything they say publicly. The FBI definitely had scared that caution into us when we went to that briefing in August. We still had to be careful what we said, but the constraints that had been tying us down since July didn't seem so heavy now. Ray and I felt so freed by this statement. It was like we had been yelling in the forest and up to this point no one had heard us. Maybe someone would believe us now.

After the rally, I checked Twitter, and my heart sank. It didn't seem like the DHS statement about the Russian responsibility for the hacking was causing much of a stir yet. I wanted the country to be as outraged as I was about this, but I supposed it might take a while for people to understand the magnitude of what it meant. The party needed to make a statement to reinforce this revelation, I thought, but I'd have to focus on that after I had some time with Bernie.

Bernie and I took a walk away from the venue. He put his hand on my back as we walked, a gesture that drew me closer to him. I was thinking that he would ask me about the hacking and that statement by DHS, but he surprised me when he started talking about Seth Rich. A few weeks earlier, a Dutch television interviewer asked Julian Assange about Seth's death. On the tape I saw of the interview, Assange fueled a conspiracy theory. He dropped his smirk and said, "Our sources take risks." Assange was implying that Seth was a source for WikiLeaks!

When the interviewer pressed him on his relationship with Seth, Assange left it vague, responding, "We do not comment on our sources. We have to understand how high the stakes are in this case."

I had been saddened by the crazy conspiracy theories that ignited on Twitter and Reddit. They wounded Seth's family. I knew this accusation was not true. As Bernie and I walked, with his steady hand on my back, he asked me about Seth's family, about his work at the DNC, and about his murder. I told him that after the second debate I was going to Nebraska to visit Seth's family and help them plan the memorial and scholarship fund. This talk with Bernie was important to me. Bernie is no-nonsense. He asks good questions, and he's always very grateful to people who tell him the truth. Sometimes when you are explaining something to a good listener you understand it better yourself. I told him my visit with Seth's family was in three days. He asked me to send them his regards, and I promised I would.

The communications staff and I were putting the final touches on our statement about the DHS announcement when I got news that the *Washington Post* had posted the *Access Hollywood* tape of Donald Trump and Billy Bush on its website.

I remember looking at it on my phone in disbelief. How much more can the public take in on a single day? I also knew that this revelation meant the DHS announcement would get next to no airtime.

I couldn't help but be distracted by the tape myself. As you surely recall, in the *Access Hollywood* tape, a bus pulls into a parking lot—a normal enough shot, it seems—and then things get disturbing as Donald Trump's commentary begins. He brags about making sexual moves on a married woman at a time when he had been married to Melania for less than a year. He leers at a woman who is standing at the entrance to the studio to greet him and talks about her legs and congratulates himself for his good luck. More than that, the way he laughs about being such a powerful man that he always gets away with whatever he does. "When you're a star you can do anything," he says.

I was disgusted by what this old man was saying, although it wouldn't have been better coming from a young one. What father talks that way? I thought of Ivanka, whom I'd gotten to know when her family was bidding on the lease for the old Post Office building on Pennsylvania Avenue, now a Trump hotel. She was elegant and well-mannered. And here was her father, a man with two daughters, saying things that any father should object to. This was sexual assault, not locker room talk. My father was a basketball player. I know many guys who play sports. I don't know anyone who talks that way.

I was certain that the GOP was finally going to unload this guy. He had turned so many tables upside down and rewritten the whole rule book, embarrassing the party many times a week, but they never left him. Finally, I thought, this was it. Trump wasn't doing very well with women in the polls, but this video would destroy even the GOP women. Every mother would think about what she would have to tell her daughter if some disgusting old man talked to her like that, and they would not stand for a party that tolerated it in the presidential candidate.

This was a game changer, if not game over. What else did we need?

As we got closer to Boston I watched the Republicans abandoning Trump. Senator after senator, congressman after congressman cited their daughters as a justification. Rep. Jason Chaffetz said if he continued to support Donald he'd never be able to look his teenage daughters in the eye again. Senator Mike Lee was so worked up he did a cell phone video denouncing Trump, thereby ruining Lee's chances for any appointment in his administration if Trump won. He must be betting, like I was, that Trump was a goner. Even Mike Pence, Trump's running mate, tried to put distance between them by saying, "I do not condone his remarks and cannot defend them. We pray for his family." The whole party, it seemed, was running in the other direction. All over Twitter and on the airwaves there was conjecture about whether or not he would be removed from the ticket.

I put out another statement: "Donald Trump's offensive, degrading, and disgusting comments about women revealed today are beyond the pale and don't bear repeating," the statement read. "The only remaining question is whether Republicans will continue to stand by him and call him a role model for our children?"

Any normal candidate would drop out of sight after a bombshell like that and spend some time with his team to figure out how to respond. Donald Trump was not going to do that. That Friday night he taped a rushed apology, but it sounded forced. He seemed angry that he had to apologize. He said he never told the world he was a perfect person, but that the tape did not reflect the man he was, and that he had changed. Those three statements don't contradict each other, but taken together they reveal a lie. Also he claimed the high road from way down in the gutter, "We are living in the real world and this is nothing more than a distraction from the real issues." And then he went after Hillary for Bill's sexual aggressions. Not the statement of a repentant man.

When I arrived at my friend Julie Goodridge's house in Jamaica Plain, she told me there was even more news that day. How had I missed it? WikiLeaks dumped 50,000 of John Podesta's emails. The Russians were doing Donald Trump another favor, releasing damaging emails to distract from the degrading things he'd said on the *Access Hollywood* tape. The emails included alleged transcripts from Hillary's speeches to Goldman Sachs. Her high speaking fees from Goldman were something Trump had been beating her up about on the campaign trail. He kept taunting her to release the speeches. And when she wouldn't, he said she had something to hide. She was telling her supporters one thing and something different to her banker pals.

In the email dump there was one paragraph where she described how we live in a global world and should lower trade barriers. WikiLeaks was intervening to save Trump's reputation once again by dumping this damaging material only a few hours after he was humiliated by the *Access Hollywood* tape. If Trump survived this disaster, I knew he would feature that statement in his stump speeches from that day forward.

I went to bed thinking he would not. His party was abandoning him, and the calls for him to resign as a candidate were coming from all corners of the country as well as the media. The combination of the DHS press release about the Russians hacking our election, along with the *Access Hollywood* tape, had guaranteed Hillary's victory. Or so I thought.

The next morning Trump rose from the swamp ready to fight us all. Paul Ryan canceled a joint fundraiser with him in Wisconsin because he didn't want to be seen on the stage next to him, but Trump didn't care. His tweets were belligerent. First he was jaunty, tweeting, *"It certainly has been an interesting 24 hours!"* Then defiant: *"The media and establishment want me out of the race so badly—I WILL NEVER DROP OUT OF THE RACE, WILL NEVER LET MY SUPPORTERS DOWN! #MAGA."*

The next move was to go after Hillary by re-tweeting remarks from Juanita Broaddrick, who has alleged that Bill had assaulted her decades before, though the case has never gone to trial. *"@atensnut: How many times must it be said? Actions speak louder than words. DT said bad things! HRC threatened me after BC raped me."* And, *"@atensnut: Hillary calls Trump's remarks "horrific" while she lives with and protects a "Rapist". Her actions are horrific."*

There was a moment there when I had to pick my head up and focus on the world outside the window. This is where we were in this election, I thought, an election that was going to decide the future of our country at a difficult time. The election that would mark for history the way we responded to electing our first black president, and this was what we were talking about. One month to go, and I didn't have any feeling that it was going to get better. I now felt that the Republicans were never going to abandon Trump no matter what he did.

From Boston I made my way to New York, where I would appear on *This Week with George Stephanopoulos* to speak about the hacking. That night would mark the second debate. George wanted to talk about the *Access Hollywood* tape and the leak of Hillary's speeches. He asked me, did I think Bernie would have won if Hillary's speech fragment had been public when she and Bernie were competing for the nomination? How could any of us know? I tried to steer the topic back to Russia.

"George, when you see something postmarked from Russia, you should be afraid to open up the document. I refuse to open these documents. I refuse to allow a foreign government . . . to interfere and meddle and manipulate information. So I don't know if it's true or not true," I said, hoping that somewhere in the living rooms of America, someone heard me.

That night, October 9, at the second presidential debate in St. Louis, the hall at Washington University was filled with tension. Had there ever been an election where both parties seriously considered replacing their candidates? I didn't remember one. Donald's plan to drown out the reverberations of the *Access Hollywood* tape was to invite three women who had accused Bill Clinton of sexually assaulting them, and one whose rapist Hillary had defended early in her legal career. He held a press conference, which the cable networks covered live, during which each of the women disparaged Hillary because of Bill and endorsed Donald Trump. Trump sat smugly with hands folded at the center of a table, two women on each side. After the women finished speaking, they stood up to leave the room without taking questions, while the reporters barked questions at Trump. I saw Steve Bannon grinning like a fool in the back, hidden among the reporters. I bet this whole stupid stunt was his idea, and the media was going for it.

The setup for the audience in St. Louis was much different from the formality of the university auditorium at Hofstra where they had held the first debate. The candidates were taking questions from the audience, who were perched on bleachers. I was on the Democratic side with Nancy Pelosi and Claire McCaskill, across from the women from the press conference who were seated near the Trump family on their side of the room.

When Hillary came out onto the stage she refused to shake Trump's hand. Maybe she was trying to insult him, or maybe she just couldn't stand the idea of touching that pussy-grabbing thing. Whatever her intent, it seemed to please him. He got feisty and he was moving around the stage with confidence, almost stalking her. As she stood at the front of the stage, he paced behind her, his large body full of fury as she addressed the crowd. I don't know how she stood her ground without flinching as he menaced her for all the world to see. He deftly threw many of the questions from the moderators and the audience back onto Hillary. When people asked him about his taxes, he bragged about not paying much, and blamed Hillary for writing the tax laws to favor her and her rich friends. Never mind that Hillary has not served in Congress, the branch of government that writes the tax laws. The zinger was clever and, for those who don't understand how government works, I bet it seemed like he won that point. But Hillary was on her game, too. She said she had faced many strong opponents, but never had she questioned anyone's fitness to serve. "Donald Trump is different," she said. No shit.

Later Hillary scored a point.

"It's good that someone with the temperament of Donald Trump is not in charge of the laws of this country," she said.

But Trump didn't miss a beat.

"Because you'd be in jail," he said. The crowd, which was told not to express reactions at these things, roared with laughter.

At the end of the debate she did shake Trump's hand, but I believe that was because she was confident that she had won. He was so far down after that sleazy tape, he needed to trounce her on the debate stage. In my opinion, he damn sure did not do that.

As I stood up to walk to the spin room I saw that it was different for this debate. We were surrounded by gossip columnists. I was interviewed by a reporter from *Inside Edition*. The campaign had become a reality television show.

I turned my phone back on. I reared back at what I saw on the screen. For the first time in this election, Donald Trump's crew had their sights trained on me. Throughout this whole campaign I had never been a target of the trolls, and I had been grateful to fly just below their radar. Since I had said those things about Donald Trump on Sunday, the insults and racial slurs had started to increase, but after my appearance on *This Week*, I had a big target on me. I watched the horrifying language and terrifying threats scroll across the phone. One said, *"How dare you present yourself as some kind of new, cleaner leadership? You have no moral standing to lead any of us. Step down now."*

And another was more direct in threatening my life.

"We've got your number, all of you," it read. *"You're going down somehow or another. If not by revolution, then by radiation sickness after your Queen starts nuclear war . . . May you lose sleep every night the way we do."*

I felt the fear rising in my body until I had to turn the face of the phone away from me. Now it was my turn in the barrel.

FIFTEEN

The Terror Comes Home

After the second debate in St. Louis, I flew to Newark and then on to Atlanta to attend a fund-raiser for the Georgia Democrats. In Atlanta I checked into the Omni Hotel, a place I had stayed at many times because it was connected to the CNN headquarters building. I was looking forward to getting some rest when I arrived, and to get my laundry done at the hotel. I had been on the road for six days and was scheduled for a few more.

At half past noon on October 11, I had been dozing when my phone rang. Rebecca Kutler, a producer from CNN, said she needed my help on a story. Just as I was answering the phone I saw an email from *Politico* and a similar one from *BuzzFeed* reporter Mary Ann Georgantopoulos, both writing about an email from the latest WikiLeaks dump. Mary Ann's read: "An email you sent Ms. Palmieri suggests you tipped off the Clinton campaign about a question a day before CNN's town hall debate in March. Did this happen? Why did you send the question? Was this allowed?"

"Do you recall CNN giving you any debate questions that you turned over to the Clinton campaign?" Rebecca asked.

I shook my head, trying to rock my brain awake so I could respond to this moment. I was stunned. Leaking questions didn't sound like something I would do. Whatever I know, I share with everybody, and besides, CNN never gave us questions in advance of one of their political events. I was searching my memory, but in this post-nap state I didn't come up with anything. I needed a clue, a time marker.

"What debate?"

She said March 12, 2016, was the date on the leaked email.

In the spring of 2016, near the beginning of the primary campaign, Bernie was gaining traction. His message of fighting for working people and the middle class resonated with both Democrats and Independents. He wanted more debates, and the DNC leadership and I agreed that there was nothing wrong with adding more.

I was a big part of the negotiations to add debates, town halls, and candidate forums. The Black Lives Matter movement was growing that spring, protesting police shootings of unarmed black men and women. They protested at campaign rallies as well as in the streets and on the freeways. Some people didn't like their tactics, but they were asking questions that the candidates needed to address. Several times my CNN colleague Van Jones and I spoke with these activists, but we were having difficulty bringing their concerns inside the CNN studios, where Trump's antics were drowning out everything. My goal in expanding the event calendar was to bring in minority moderators and air the events in partnership with minority-owned networks. I was in daily contact with all the campaigns, the party, and the candidates to develop ideas for topics to include in the debate. But sharing debate questions? I couldn't remember sharing any questions with any of them.

Rebecca said the email subject line was: "From time to time I get the questions in advance."

What? That was impossible. CNN never gave us the questions in advance. Plus that subject line—bragging like that— did not sound like me. I searched my iPad and my iPhone, but I couldn't locate an email with that subject line on either of those. Maybe it was on my laptop computer at home, I told Rebecca. I had six or seven email addresses: private ones from my cable provider and my Gmail, three business addresses, a government one, a university one, and a political one. With all these, I usually got six hundred emails a day. At home I could search all of those for any email with that heading.

Still, I couldn't be sure that my home computer held the answer. In June 2016, the IT team at the DNC technicians wiped all emails connected with any device they did not consider to be secure. Did the emails from that time survive on my home computer? I didn't know. Rebecca, my producer and my boss at CNN, didn't seem too concerned. This was merely housekeeping, she told me. She assured me it would all blow over soon. I went off to the fund-raiser.

When I checked my phone again at two thirty, the story of my alleged terrible deed was all over the Internet. My jaw dropped. People from the left and the right had the long knives out for me, and it hurt to see how everyone suddenly wanted to take me down. Those from the Trump side emphasized how I was part of the "media elite" and in the tank for Hillary, and so did the Bernie Bros. As much as I respected Bernie, I was exhausted by the self-righteousness of the Bernie Bros. Bernie came into the race as an outsider who had criticized the Democratic Party. Nonetheless, the party embraced him. It worked with him to make sure he was on the ballot. He had legitimate reasons to complain about the actions of a handful of people at the DNC, and I had been totally forthcoming to him about that. But overall the game was not rigged against him. He knew this and has said as much, but his staunchest supporters refused to accept it. Now I was becoming their target.

Rebecca sent me the allegedly leaked email, dated March 12, 2016, which started:

> Here's one that worries me about HRC.
> DEATH PENALTY
> 19 states and the District of Columbia have banned the death penalty. 31 states, including Ohio, still have the death penalty. According to the National Coalition to Abolish the Death Penalty, since 1973, 156 people have been on death row and later set free. Since 1976, 1,414 people have been executed in the U.S. That's 11% of Americans who were sentenced to die, but later exonerated and freed. Should Ohio and the 30 other states join the current list and abolish the death penalty?

I didn't recall that email, but I did remember that time. My friend Roland Martin, whom I had worked with at CNN, was having a big moment then. He was about to comoderate a town hall with Jake Tapper at Ohio State University. He and I were brainstorming what questions he should ask Bernie and Hillary this weekend before primaries in six states. I wanted to bring up important issues about race and inequality so that both candidates could speak to them. That question was one of those that had made the cut. Roland and I had been tossing around ideas all week long, but I still didn't recall sharing questions with Hillary's campaign.

With the pressure growing, Rebecca needed answers. I suggested she just put me on air, seeing as I was in a hotel right next door to the CNN studios. Rebecca said they didn't want me on right then. By the next time she called, an hour later, I had begun to understand how this controversy now threatened to overtake the week's news cycle. I canceled my hotel reservation and after my event at Georgia State and a fund-raiser for the Georgia Democrats flew standby to DC so I could get to my desktop computer.

Two things motivated this abrupt change in plans. I became increasingly worried that the Trump campaign would use this WikiLeaks dump to sow discord between the Sanders and Clinton supporters. The other was fear of how Donald Trump would exploit this to further attack Hillary's integrity. I would be his latest villain. To him this was further proof of how the Clinton family secretly pulled the levers of power, how she controlled the media. He would repeat my name over and over in his evening rallies. When Trump linked my name to hers, the harassment would become a category five. As the cab was pulling up in front of the airport, Rebecca called me again. CNN had decided to release a statement abandoning me and any responsibility for this action. The network said that it never had shared questions with me and, since the question came to CNN the day after it appeared in my email, this was my dilemma.

"Please don't do this," I begged her. "You don't have all the facts. What if it's not true? How can you trust it?"

She said it wasn't her decision. She just wanted me to know.

"Rebecca, please, no," I said. "Hold off for just a little while. You do this, you're putting my life at risk. Please."

Again, not her call.

On the flight I tried to calm myself down, but one glass of wine was not enough. On the second glass I got a little maudlin, reassuring myself that I had value in this world. I steadied myself by thinking about how much I value fairness. I know those who have worked with me would agree this is something I exhibit in my actions.

As we flew north, I moved from doubt to resignation. What was I rushing home for? The truth did not matter. The accusa-

tion had more power than the refutation. And if I did locate the
email, everyone's worst idea of me would seem true. From his
treatment of women to his refusal to release his tax returns, we
seemed incapable of landing any criticism on Trump for his outrageous behavior. But now I would be a punching bag. I was the
liar, the cheat, and the thief. And if I could not find that email,
that would not exonerate me. My enemies would maintain that I
was covering it up. True or not, I was going to be humiliated. It
didn't matter whether or not CNN released the statement.

By the time I landed I moved from self-absorption to for-
giveness. My friends at CNN were under attack, too. Trump was
mocking them, mocking all of the press. At his rallies he put the
press in a pen in the middle of the auditorium and invited his
supporters to boo at them and throw things. He had a special
dark spot in his heart for CNN. They were his most frequent
media target. As a result, the network was under enormous pressure. The smallest mistake triggered furious backlash, as Trump
used it to whip his acolytes and Internet trolls into a frenzy.

I realized I needed to resign as I was likely to be fired. This
made me sad. It was heartbreaking that I had to part with CNN
under these circumstances. I had loved working there for fourteen years. I respected the professionalism of my colleagues and
felt fortunate to have lasted as long as I had. Resigning now
would take some of the pressure off. It was one of the many
things I would have to straighten out after the election, when
heads were cooler.

When I got off the plane, I was grateful to see Mr. Singh standing there, waiting to drive me. I had been arguing with Patrice
about using Mr. Singh, who did most of the driving for the DNC.
I didn't want all that fuss and trappings, but Patrice would not
budge on this issue. I knew she was right when Mr. Singh took
my heavy carry-on and my backpack out of my arms and got

my luggage from the carousel. As he drove me home, I emailed my resignation to CNN. Then I started tweeting compliments about the network and some of the fine people I'd worked with. They had given me a platform, always treating me with respect. I knew the gracious thing to do was to acknowledge that in these personal tweets to my colleagues. Looking back on this now, I'm surprised I could concentrate on this task.

I was relieved to be home, though, even with the controversy raging. I refused Mr. Singh's offer to bring my luggage upstairs. I was thinking how the next day I'd see Kai when I went to Betsy and Mia's to bring my dog, Chip, back home. I was smiling at that happy thought but a moment later my smile vanished. As I got to the top of the stairs I saw a white object sitting on the side of the front porch. I stopped to look at the package, but immediately backed away. It was crumpled and about eight by six inches with bugs crawling all over it and Bernie's name scrawled on the top.

Mr. Singh, who had not yet reached his car door, heard me gasp and cuss, and then saw me step back. He came running up the stairs and we both stood to the side staring at this thing. I wondered what was in that bag. Mr. Singh took a picture of it with his cell phone, but neither of us wanted to go anywhere near it. My porch was up a long flight of stairs from the street level. No one could have dropped this thing by accident while walking by.

Mr. Singh made sure I got safely into the house, but then I didn't know whom I should call. Should I call the police? Should I call Besty and Mia? It was past midnight now. I kept peeking out the French door to look at the package, like it was going to move. I didn't know what to do. I turned on every light in the house and walked around checking to see if anything was different from when I left. I knew I would not be able to sleep. I popped some popcorn and opened a bottle of wine. At 4:30 a.m. my Spook called.

His habit was to call me when the Russians had gone off duty for the evening. This was when he'd check in with his spooky friends to report to me if they had detected much activity from them on the web. This time he heard the fear in my voice. When I told him about the suspicious package on my front step, his tone changed from confidential to serious.

"Do you have a pet?"

"Yes, I have Chip, my dog, but he's been staying with my friends while I was away."

"Maybe you should leave him with your friends until the election is over."

"Oh no! I don't want to do that. I need him. I mean, he's my little Boo! Someone for me to talk to when I get home at night."

"I know. I appreciate that. But sometimes the Russians go after a target's pets. They are good with poison. They might try to poison Chip. What do you think was in that package? Was it food?"

"I didn't get too close to it, but it looked like donuts."

"Like I said, I think it's best that you let your friends take care of Chip."

I agreed, and I felt so sad. This was for the best, and it hurt.

The next morning I called a man who does odd jobs for me around the house—Mr. Dobson—to come take the package away. He said the package did contain spoiled food. I was relieved it wasn't anything worse, but I still felt violated. Whoever put it there despised me—and knew where I lived.

I went over to see Kai and to tell Betsy and Mia that I needed them to keep Chip until the election was over. Mia, a Navy vet, recommended I have a security team come to sweep the house and look for vulnerabilities. She was talking a mile a minute about where to place cameras and motion-sensitive lights, but

I was only half-hearing her. She saw that, so she got online and found cameras for every window, motion-sensitive lights, and a controller for it all that would send live pictures from the cameras to my iPad.

My mind was in a million places. I was thinking about my reputation, built on more than forty years in politics. I had been unable to find that email on my home computer, but that would not be a sufficient answer to my critics. I saw email chains where Roland had reached out to many friends and listeners asking for suggestions for topics at the town hall. I sent him several issues, including one on the death penalty. He sent those questions on to CNN—they didn't come through me. I saw that I had shared potential topics for that event with Bernie's camp, too. I found it odd that I would reach out to John Podesta through Jennifer Palmieri, as I have a direct line of communication with John. It all seemed like an election fable, like many that had been cooked up to confuse the voters about the integrity of the election.

If I had made this mistake, I would own it. But, given all the fishy business of this election, I would have to look further into it to convince myself that I had really done this. But I knew that— no matter what—there was no chance of clearing my name now.

Stories about me and the email were on every news site and cable show now. Donald Trump had tweeted about me the night before: *"Wow, @CNN Town Hall questions were given to Crooked Hillary Clinton in advance of big debates against Bernie Sanders. Hillary & CNN FRAUD!"*

He started using this allegation at his rallies, as I knew he would. At a rally in West Palm Beach, Florida, he said: "Honestly, she should be locked up. Should be locked up. And likewise the emails show that the Clinton machine is so closely and irrevocably tied to the media organizations that she, listen to this, is given the questions and answers in advance of her debate performance with Bernie Sanders. Hillary Clinton is also given approval and veto power over quotes written about her in the *New York Times*. And the emails show the reporters conspire and collaborate with helping her win the election."

This was crazy talk, and I was embarrassed that I was part of it. I didn't want to add fuel to this inferno. The Clinton campaign was holding steady in its policy of never commenting on or validating any information that was released by Guccifer, DCLeaks or WikiLeaks. No one in the party said I should resign as interim chair, but no one from the campaign came to my defense, either. Perhaps they understood that this was a hit job. Most of the messages I got were private, from colleagues saying they were praying for me, that I should ignore this and go forward. I had no obligation to answer this charge, but I felt badly even if I agreed with those people who were encouraging me to hang tough. I didn't know where to go. I didn't want to go home and I didn't want to go into the office. This whole situation unmoored me, and I didn't know when it would end.

The next day, even Jake Tapper took a swing at me, calling me unethical and "journalistically horrifying," during a radio interview with WMAL even though I worked for CNN as a commentator, not a journalist. When I called him on this, he did not apologize. His attack on me was really about him. He wrote in an email, "I don't know what happened here except it undermines the integrity of my work and CNN . . . you have to know how betrayed we all feel."

The feeling is mutual, my friend.

I decided I needed to take evasive action for my safety. I began taking a different route home every night. Often I stopped off at Betsy and Mia's to see Kai and Chip, but I drove way out of my way to confuse anyone who might be following me. I alerted the DC police, too, asking them if they would tell the patrol officers to swing by my house a little more often. I also asked my neighbors to keep an eye on my house. If there was a car parked in front of it for very long, would they please write down the license plate for me? Maybe they could take a picture of it too, just for my files.

By the end of the week the DNC had hired a security firm to sweep the house and help me analyze where I needed a security upgrade. The technician brought twelve huge metal cases into my living room that contained electronic equipment to scan for frequency irregularities on my cable and Internet service and my phones. He also looked for listening devices on the outside and inside. He asked me first where I spent most of my time. I said, "In my boobatoir." He didn't know what I was talking about. That's a New Orleans word I've heard nowhere else. The boobatoir is that room of the house where you lay down and binge-watch television. It's the place where you kick off your shoes and set down your purse after a long day. Mine had a comfy sofa and a nice big television.

I watched him scanning it with his devices. Up and down the cables and the windowsills, the doorjambs, and even the floorboards. His verdict was that this was the room that was the most vulnerable. It had so many windows. (That was why I liked it.) There were two entrances to the room—from the house and from the porch—so that made it less secure. He recommended thousands of dollars of security upgrades, and that I spend a lot less time in my boobatoir.

The day the team came to install the security system I felt so ruined by this whole election. Just as Mia had recommended, I now had cameras trained on every window and door of my house and motion-sensitive lighting on pathways and in the garage. The security team at the DNC were wary for me, too. They installed a special camera at my parking space so they could monitor if anyone was tampering with my car. Donald Trump had created this madness. His philosophy was either rule or ruin, so he was trying to ruin me. He had turned thousands of my fellow citizens, people who never knew me and never would, against me.

Every morning when I got into work, there were threatening messages from people saying they were coming to get me and that they would make me answer for this. After I made my long and winding way home, the messages on my home line were even more frightening. When I was campaigning for President Obama, strangers had called me a nigger and made all manner of other insults about my race. Now, as I advocated for Hillary, the threats had become even more violent and personal. They knew where I lived, they'd say, and I shouldn't get too comfortable. Maybe I shouldn't go to sleep at night because I might not wake up. I had shut all the curtains and drawn all the blinds in my house. There was no Chip for me to snuggle with at night, and I stopped spending time in my garden. I remember standing at the back door looking out with sadness. The plants were growing wildly, weeds starting to make their way up among the flowers, and animals were nibbling on my vegetables. It was hot, but I did not feel safe enough to go out there and water my plants.

I needed help but I did not know where I could turn.

SIXTEEN

State of Denial

To get the help I needed, I ended up turning to an unlikely source: the Republicans. I'm not kidding when I say that. In the months since the convention, as I gained a greater command of the situation at the DNC and the world of hacking, I understood the importance of both parties coming out in support of free and fair elections. The hacking was not just a new technique in the high stakes world of American politics. The DNC had suffered a break-in that was putting our democracy at risk. If the GOP and the Democrats made a joint statement objecting to a foreign power meddling in our electoral process, it would be a lot stronger than if the Democrats made that statement alone.

It seemed like a no-brainer to ask both parties to issue a joint statement underscoring the importance of honest elections. That earlier statement from the seventeen intelligence agencies who all agreed with high confidence that the Russians had hacked the DNC should be proof enough for any American. Yet the people I knew who were high up in the GOP and the campaign refused my emails and my calls when I pleaded with them to

join me in condemning these acts of cyber terrorism. Apparently
they saw it as good for their side, and that was all that mattered.

Sean Spicer was a gossip buddy of mine before he was Trump's
first press secretary. I had his email and his cell number from
all the Saturdays he called me before I appeared on CNN and
ABC's Sunday shows to talk about politics. At that time he
was the communications director for the Republican National
Committee. I'd usually be in my cab on the way to my hotel
when I'd see Sean's name on my phone, and I would know what
he wanted, what he always wanted: to know what topics the producers told me we would discuss when I joined the round table
that next morning with George Stephanopoulos.

Sean is a guy with a great sense of humor—and the kind of
guy who knew that if I was going to give him something, he had
to give me something in return. I'd share the topics, and from
him I'd get some little inside tidbit about the goings-on on his
side of the street. We're old political hands. We know the drill.
I knew that when he spoke, his voice would make it sound like
he was divulging a big secret, but most likely he was just trying
to plant something in my ear that he hoped I might use when
it was my turn to speak. Now that I was no longer a pundit,
our Saturday conversations had stopped. Communicating as we
had before would not be right, now that we were political opponents. The hacking of the election was something that, for me,
was above the partisan divide. It was not for Sean, though.

I texted him. I emailed him. I brought it up when we were
face-to-face at the debates, but I could see his eyes dart away like
this was the last thing he wanted to talk to me about. He would
slap me on the shoulder like the warm acquaintances that we
were, and move as quickly as he could away from me.

Same thing with Reince Priebus, the chair of the Republican
Party. Reince and I were well acquainted. He had clashed with

Debbie when she was chair. If he needed to cut a deal with the party about not scheduling our primary candidate debates on the same day, or if both of us wanted to take a stand on a state's primary rules, he called me and I brought the issue to Debbie or to the party leadership to see what we could do to get it resolved. This had built mutual respect, and I was trading on that positive past when I approached him about making a joint statement about the election.

I was not expecting a frosty reception when I walked up to Reince at the vice presidential debate, trying desperately to follow up on the text messages I'd been sending him about making a joint statement about the election. I didn't get a really frosty reception, I got that special DC frost where the person smiles when he sees you but immediately looks past you trying to find someone in the room to come right over and interrupt the conversation. I saw his eyes searching around the room even as he was drawing me a little close for an anemic hug.

"How ya doing, Donna?"

"Fine, I'm doing fine. How *you* doing?"

"Doing well. It's a crazy time."

"So Reince, I wanted to talk to you about the texts I sent you last week. We really need to say that both parties are against the Russians' hacking of our elections. You agree, don't you?"

"Hey, Donna, it's good to see you but I've got to talk to that guy from *Politico*."

So thanks for nothing, zip, nada. I was desperate to get a briefing on this topic from the Department of Homeland Security, which had indicated it had information to share about the election, but the department wanted to brief representatives from both parties simultaneously. The Republicans apparently were not interested in taking this meeting. We tried to schedule it many times over the course of six weeks, but they wouldn't commit.

In the meantime, Donald Trump was treating the drip, drip, drip of our personal emails as his opposition research, not ill-gotten gains of a crime. He hammered away on Twitter, saying that the information from WikiLeaks proved that Hillary was a criminal and should be locked up. On October 16 he tweeted: *"We all wondered how Hillary avoided prosecution for her email scheme. WikiLeaks may have found the answer. Obama!"* He then tweeted on October 17: *"Crooked Hillary colluded w/FBI and DOJ and media is covering up to protect her. It's a #RiggedSystem! Our country deserves better!"* He still did not let up the next day, the day before the last candidate's debate, when he tweeted: *"Hillary is the most corrupt person to ever run for the presidency of the United States. #DrainTheSwamp!"* He was gleeful about the invasion of our privacy. One website tallied that he mentioned WikiLeaks 164 times in the month of October.

My alleged leaking of the questions to Hillary before one of the Democratic candidate forums continued to be a big theme in Trump's tweets and his rallies. *"Voter fraud! Crooked Hillary Clinton even got the questions to a debate, and nobody says a word. Can you imagine if I got the questions?"* he tweeted October 17. From the rally stage he always mentioned me, and always as if I were second only to "Crooked Hillary" in infamy for this thing I very well might not have done. The death threats and terrorizing phone calls escalated the more he mentioned me.

I knew I needed to get to the bottom of whether or not I had given questions to Hillary—and Hillary only—in advance of the CNN/TV One–sponsored town hall forum in March, in which she would face Bernie Sanders. (Martin O'Malley had dropped out of the race right after the Iowa caucuses.) In a way, my life depended on it. In the days after my return home, I searched my memory for a recollection of writing the email. I also searched through all the emails on my office computer for Brazile and

Associates, but I could not come up with a subject line that said "sometimes I get the questions in advance." I asked my assistant to get a technician who could go through the server to see if any fragments of that email remained, but he found nothing. I called Roland Martin, who was not very happy to hear from me. We had worked so well together during his six years as a contributor at CNN and since. That happy collaboration we had forged over the years had now dragged him into this mess, and he was upset with me about that, despite the fact that he couldn't find the email in question in his files, either.

Roland and I had both been unhappy with the lack of discussion on issues specific to black Americans during the primary season. He and I talked frequently and often lamented the debate moderators failing to raise these issues that were so important to one of the Democratic Party's most crucial constituencies.

Roland knew these issues mattered. He is the host of a national daily morning show targeting African Americans on TV One, and, in October 2015, he had questioned Hillary Clinton at one of her town halls in South Carolina, on the campus of a historically black college. He spent months, to no avail, trying to get Bernie Sanders to do a similar one.

What Roland and I wanted for the upcoming CNN/TV One–sponsored forum was to ensure that issues important to people of color, such as the justice system and the disproportionate number of our citizens who were in jail and on death row, were included. As Roland later told his TV One audience, he had been discussing these issues with many others, bouncing ideas off of professors he knew at historically black and Ivy League universities, with prominent Black Lives Matter activists, and other black political figures, like me.

I came to believe that the email contained some of the ideas that I had been tossing back and forth with Roland, similar to the way I had once shared topics I was going to talk about on the

ABC Sunday shows with Sean Spicer. The reason that the networks paid me, and many party operatives like me, to comment
on the news of the day was that I was plugged into a world of
insiders. Forty years in politics gave me a contact list and a perspective that went below the surface, deep into the places where
the media could not see. In that world, information is a form of
currency, and we all trade it back and forth all the time.

The death penalty was a topic that no one had raised in the
primary debates and forums preceding the one with Roland
Martin and Jake Tapper. Assuming the email was legitimate,
I would have thought that I didn't want any of our candidates
blindsided by this turn of subject matter. But what I could
not accept was that I would have shared information with one
Democratic candidate and not the other. My rule was that when
I shared something, I shared it with everyone. I know that if I
shared anything for the debate with Hillary's team, I also shared
it with Bernie's. If Martin O'Malley were still in the race, I would
have shared it with his team, too.

The Clinton people had remained silent on this matter, and
that really hurt. Not one of them stood up for me on air. The
people who were coming to my defense were the Bernie people.
Bernie's chief strategist, Tad Devine, said on Andrea Mitchell's
midday show that I had always treated them fairly and so did
his campaign manager, Jeff Weaver. It wasn't quite exoneration
from the Bernie camp, but it made me feel a little better.

The policy of the campaign and the party was to refuse to verify, or even discuss, the stolen materials published by WikiLeaks,
DCLeaks, and Guccifer, but it was clear that a portion of it had
been doctored in some way. Jake Tapper's claim in his email that
none of the emails had been revealed to be phony was just igno-
rance on his part, and seemed to be motivated by his fury at
me. On August 2, right after the convention, *New York Times*

reporter Yamiche Alcindor received an email purporting to be from our press secretary, Mark Paustenbach, pitching her what it called an "Opted" (a misspelling of *op-ed*, or opinion piece) for the paper's editorial page, saying also that I would be sending the piece along shortly.

When Yamiche responded to Mark that she would contact the editorial page editors, Mark was taken aback. He hadn't sent an op-ed email to anyone. It was bogus. Right after that, she received an email from one of my addresses, offering Yamiche a ludicrous essay that allegedly had been written by Tim Kaine about how the vice president's job was to make the president look good. It read, "It's like when you go to a club, and you see those hot girls next to their boring ugly friends. I'm the boring ugly friend. I'm the one that doesn't get drugged at the bar, because no one wants to touch me with a fifty-foot pole." I still laugh, thinking anyone would believe those words could come from Tim.

I was familiar with how the Russians could take over your email and start sending phony messages. On the evening of October 12, a few days after I was accused of leaking that question to Hillary, I'd gotten an email that appeared to be from John Podesta's account. The subject was "We have a problem" and it read:

> Donna, some of our less than reliable media people are starting to privately question the Russian hack story we've been feeding them about these emails that Assange keeps leaking. We're worried they may start questioning it not so privately. You know as well as I do if the media starts slamming her on this it'll take coverage off Trump.
>
> HRC wants us to come up with a backup story to keep them guessing until we get to E-day in case we need to use it. Do you have any ideas? We know we can count on you, Donna.

Are you kidding me? This ploy was so absurd. As if Russia was a phony story! I knew how Podesta sounds, and I knew this was not him. I forwarded the fake email to the security team to check against our email database, and I also alerted some people at Hillary for America, who were certain that it was fake. To me, it was evidence that some of the DNC emails were fakes. Someone was trying to make people doubt that the election was fair, and Donald Trump was seizing on it. As Trump campaigned in October, his major theme was that the system was rigged, and my email controversy fed into the narrative he was running with.

As I frantically searched for proof that would restore my reputation, it dawned on me that I was in a no-win position. It appeared that I had violated some cardinal sin of journalism in appearing to favor one side over the other. Whatever the facts, it was the appearance that mattered. I knew there was no way that any of the people who questioned me on television would be interested in a long and nuanced explanation. That world is quick. The questions would be: *Did you do it or not? And are you sorry?* If I didn't have a snappy comeback, I'd get cut off and expose myself to further ridicule. The best, if regrettable, course of action was to take the hits now and reconcile with my accusers after the election.

And the hits were coming from all sides. They were digging up emails I'd written about Obama in 2009 saying that people were still hurting under his economy. They published this as if it had been written in 2016. Where was this coming from? And why did the emails they dropped seem to support perfectly the talking points Trump had for that day's campaign?

The attacks were unrelenting and coming on several fronts at once. On October 17, that sleazy Republican operative James O'Keefe released a doctored video that showed Scott Foval, who worked for one of the campaign contractors, boasting about paying protestors to incite violence at Trump rallies.

The violence at Trump rallies was becoming a big issue. Trump would stand on the stage and rile up the worst in people with his incitements to throw Muslims out of the country, and his long narratives about Hillary and how the system was rigged against him and his supporters. He told the crowds it was time to take the country back. If they stuck with him, he would restore them and their families to power. Protestors who were brave enough to get into Trump rallies were sometimes beaten by his supporters, punched in the face, and always humiliated. The media, penned in as they were and also subjects of Trump's ire, talked about how dangerous this was, and they saw it as a reflection of the dark mood in the country. When James O'Keefe produced this footage, Trump gloated that he and his supporters were not to blame. It was all coming from Crooked Hillary.

I watched O'Keefe's video with a sinking heart, knowing this was something we could not fight back against, not really. Every political campaign has an operation that sends out people to their opponents' campaign events to make sure that the media and the participants also get a dose of the opposition point of view. The people who take on this work might be union members with signs for their candidate or people with flyers to hand out to those waiting to enter the venue, and might even be that Damn Duck. In the budget the term we use for it is *bracketing*. We hire a contractor, like Bob Creamer, to do this work of organizing the opposition force, and also to organize rallies for our candidates. The Republicans do it, too. In 2016, this program conducted hundreds of press events. None of them involved any violence whatsoever.

Regardless, the footage of Foval boasting about picking fights with crazy people in the line to a campaign rally looked terrible. Foval was taped saying, "It doesn't matter what the fricking legal and ethics people say. We need to win this mother fucker . . . In the lines at Trump rallies, we're starting anarchy."

Creamer confidently said that Hillary was definitely aware of what he was doing with the duck. "The campaign is fully in it," Creamer said. "Hillary knows through the chain of command." Foval described in detail how money could flow through different contractors and PACs so that it could not be traced directly to the campaign.

I knew how much fuel this would add to the raging fire of this campaign. What he had captured in this doctored video did not look doctored, and it also captured everything that the voters suspect about the corruption of politics. Voters would see this as proof that they were being manipulated by powerful forces who saw them as pawns in a high-level scam.

How did they get it? That was something everyone in the party and the campaign wanted to know. I was part of a long email chain between the campaign, the party, and many contractors on the day that the video was released about how the young woman who took the surreptitious footage got in.

She called herself "Angela Brandt," and she had passed herself off as the niece of a friend of Bob Creamer who wanted to volunteer at Mike Lux's office to work on the bracketing operation. Later we discovered her real name was Allison Maass, a woman who had infiltrated Hillary's campaign in Iowa and was caught by Russ Feingold's senate campaign in Wisconsin before she caused any trouble there. At Mike Lux's office she moved in undetected. Quickly she had a key card and access to the email system there. Mike said she'd only used the key card twice, which meant every other time she was at the office she was surrounded by others. That also meant that two times she was there alone, able to do whatever she pleased. She even came to the DNC, as part of that team from Mike's office. The day that someone from the Sinclair Broadcast Group confronted Bob Creamer about the footage, she folded up her laptop, gathered her personal items, and walked out the door without saying a word to anyone.

Here we were in the middle of an election where our security was daily under threat, and this kind of foolishness, this lack of concern for vetting volunteers, took place. I wanted someone else to deal with it, but I knew I would take the hit to deflect from a focus on the campaign. That's what principals do. Whether it was true or not, it was something else that would be hung around my neck as the chair of the DNC when both sides gathered for the final debate in Las Vegas in two days.

Before I left for Las Vegas we had our long-delayed meeting with the Department of Homeland Security. The GOP still declined to join us, so just a few people from the DNC and HFA went. The meeting reflected what Pratt Wiley, the director of the DNC Voting Rights Institute, was hearing about attempts to break into the electronic voting system in Arizona and Georgia, and perhaps other states that had not realized it yet. The DHS also was picking up on Russian attempts to infiltrate the electronic voting systems in several states. The DHS was working with any secretary of state who would cooperate to determine if the Russians had been successful, but it was getting rebuffed by many of them who suspected federal interference in the election process. I worried that our system—and whatever way it might be connected to those voting systems—might be a route in.

When the people who were giving us the briefing warned about more dire attacks, like a Russian attempt to take down the power grid on Election Day, I felt as though I had reached my saturation point. With the attacks on my home, and me, the DNC, the mole in our office, the terror in the faces of the people I held dear, and now this plot to hack the vote itself, it was all too much. As we drove back to the DNC, I joked that I wanted to put crime scene tape around that building. There were so many crimes being committed against us in that building, and perhaps there were even more that we had yet to uncover.

As I was preparing to fly to Las Vegas for the last debate, Julie, Patrice, and Anne took me aside. They were worried about me traveling alone. The attacks on me had become so frequent and so vicious that they preferred that I have someone along who would watch out for me. What they did not know was how I had been cautioning my family that they should be extra careful now. Our name, Brazile, was distinctive, and it would have been easy for my many sisters and brothers and their children to become the target of some crazed person out to harm me. Several of my siblings said they wanted to come stay with me just until Election Night to make sure I was safe, but I told them no. All I could think about was Seth Rich. Had he been killed by someone who had it out for the Democrats? Likely not, but we still didn't know. If they came after me like that, I didn't want anyone else to get hurt. This became a very heated conversation. I wanted to maintain my autonomy and not to cause anyone harm, but my colleagues were genuinely concerned for my well-being. Anne mentioned several people who had agreed to escort me, but I instructed her to thank those people and reaffirm that I would travel alone.

The debate was in a basketball stadium, the Thomas & Mack Center at the University of Nevada, Las Vegas, on October 19. Before the start of the broadcast, I went around and said hello to everybody, but especially I wanted to talk to Reince. The day after the DHS meeting I sent him a formal letter on DNC stationary offering that we be briefed together on the hacking of the DNC so that he would know what had happened to us. I didn't expect him to believe me, but he might believe the Department of Homeland Security. I still wanted him to work with me on a joint statement about assuring the integrity of the elections. When I went over to him before the debate, he managed to wiggle out of the conversation once again.

When we all entered the arena and I saw where I was seated, I burst out laughing. I was no longer among those seated in the front row or among the family. I was not even visible. They had seated me in bleachers behind the scrim that served as the back-drop to the debate stage so that no one in the audience or the cameras could see. That was where they put me and the Rev. Jesse Jackson, among others whom they had to invite but wanted to tuck away. I would have seen more of this debate if I'd stayed home. The only thing I could see was the back of the monitors.

I was tired. It had gotten to the point that the only time I could sleep was when I was in an airplane. When I was up in the air, I knew they couldn't get to me. I was cut off from the threats, the insults, and the daily drama. As soon as I smelled the jet fuel fumes, I started to nod off and rapidly fell asleep. This was part of the reason I didn't want anyone to travel with me. I needed those few hours of rest. When I recognized this slight, I decided to make the best of it. When you are in the front row, you have to be careful how you behave because the camera could be on you at any minute, especially if you rolled your eyes. Here in the back with the outliers, I could eat mints and chew bubble gum and even nod off if it got boring.

It was not boring. Hillary was great, wearing suffragette white, confident and glowing. Trump was full of rage and con-descension, as if he didn't want to go through this again because she had beaten him so badly the other two times. The contempt they had for each other was obvious. They didn't even shake hands before they stood behind the podiums. Chris Wallace, who was the moderator, made sure to announce in advance that he and he alone had written the questions and decided what they would be. I was too tired to see that as an insult to me, even if it was, and also a portent of what was to come.

She took him on with grace and was never intimidated by his smirking bluster. The highlight for me was when Hillary stood him down on the hacking of the election. Chris Wallace asked her a question about one of the speeches she allegedly had made that was published by our old enemy WikiLeaks. In it she talked about open borders for trade and advocated for a global electrical grid. On the debate stage she acknowledged she supported that, but quickly pivoted to ask him to doubt it because of the questionable source of the information:

> You are very clearly quoting from WikiLeaks, and what is really important about WikiLeaks is that the Russian government has engaged in espionage against Americans. They have hacked American websites and American accounts of private people, of institutions. Then they have given that information to WikiLeaks for the purpose of putting it on the Internet. This has come from the highest levels of the Russian government, clearly from Putin himself, in an effort, as seventeen of our intelligence agencies have confirmed, to influence our election. So I actually think the most important question of this evening, Chris, is finally: Will Donald Trump admit and condemn that the Russians are doing this, and make it clear that he will not have the help of Putin in this election, that he rejects Russian espionage against Americans, which he actually encouraged in the past?

Trump mocked her for the pivot from open borders to Putin, and the crowd laughed. Chris Wallace had to admonish the audience not to react audibly.

Later, of the hacks, Trump repeated his claim—despite the unanimous agreement of seventeen nonpartisan government agencies—that we had "no idea" if the perpetrator was "Russia, China or anybody else."

Hillary shot back that Trump "would rather believe Vladimir Putin than the military and civilian intelligence professionals who are sworn to protect us."

For me, this was the best answer she could have given, and I admired how she baited him into that trap. It was not clear that the crowd was with her on this, but I hoped and prayed that some people in the television audience were.

When it was over, I made my way with Adam Hodge, the DNC communications director, to the spin room. There was a pen where the featured guests of the two parties were supposed to gather to take questions from the press, who were straining at the barriers with their cameras and recording devices. In the pen were Mike Pence, Reince Priebus, Jennifer Palmieri, and that snake James O'Keefe, who had made all those fraudulent videos to spread bad information about the DNC. Why was that guy in the pen, protected by Pence's secret service? I was too tired to get angry. I wanted to do my duty to talk about how great Hillary was and get back to the hotel. One of my last prebooked interviews was with Megyn Kelly for Fox. It was less of an interview than an ambush. She was so eager to get to me that when she saw me approaching, her producers yanked Trump campaign manager Kellyanne Conway out of the chair almost midsentence so I could sit down right away. Megyn was gunning for me.

I expected to talk about the fact that Trump would not commit in advance to whether or not he would accept the result of the election, but Megyn was having none of that. She wanted to talk about paid protestors and James O'Keefe, and she wanted to talk about me leaking questions to Hillary.

On half the screen was footage of the violence that broke out at a Trump rally in Chicago in March. This spooled out while Megyn asked me about Bob Creamer's contract with the DNC. All I could say was that the contract existed before I took over as chair, and now it had been terminated and all others involved had been fired. This was not enough for Megyn, who wanted me to own this, admit to it, apologize for it, and make more footage for Fox to display. I was not fast on my feet that day. I didn't have my usual wry smile and quick capacity to turn the subject around. I tried to praise Hillary for her great debate performance, but Megyn was impatient with me because she wanted to attack me about the debate question. I felt my shoulders slump as she laid into me with such fury.

"As a Christian woman I understand persecution, but I will not sit here and be persecuted because your information is totally false," I said. "What you're telling the American people—"

"I'm getting this from Podesta's emails."

"But Podesta's emails were stolen," I said.

"So you deny it? CNN's Jake Tapper said that this was unethical. Someone was unethically helping the Clinton campaign."

I tried to explain that I had my records, that this was falsified, that I never in my life had gotten a debate question in advance from CNN, but her impatience with me only grew. The minute I tried to defend myself, she looked as bored as bored could be, and rushed me off camera. She had gotten what she wanted from those ten minutes attacking me. I was too numb, too tired, from the whole thing to cry, and when I looked around the spin room for a familiar shoulder to collapse upon, there was no one there. Not a single Democrat or Democratic pundit left in the space. I wanted so bad for this whole thing to be over, but there were still three weeks to go.

That night, Donald Trump took the time to tweet, linking to a clip of Kelly's interview with me:

"Totally dishonest Donna Brazile chokes on the truth. Highly illegal!"

SEVENTEEN

Firefighters

The week the Hacker House team started to arrive, in the beginning of October, we established a routine of twice-a-day phone calls to keep us up-to-date on what they found as they dropped into the compromised maze of the DNC computer system.

The calls included Heather Adkins, who seemed to be an angel of cyberspace, floating around the globe as she managed a global team of security engineers for her employer. No matter what time zone she was in, Heather always was available to help. Nicole Wong was on the calls, too, even though her expertise was policy. She could not do the work that the Hacker House team did but she, unlike me, understood everything they said. And although I didn't know the jargon, what I got from participating in these calls was a jolt of the bright energy of Hacker House. I could feel it without understanding all the technical ins and outs.

The Hacker House crew were outsiders to the toxic culture of Washington, DC, patriots who brought their big brains to this problem because they wanted to make sure that the election was a fair fight. Rob Witoff told me as much. "There is nothing political about this for me," he said. "This is not about who wins. If a foreign power is interfering with our election, I want to prevent that." They operated in the world inside those hundreds of servers and laptops connected to our scattered network and spoke the language of the thousands of lines of code that they needed to review in order to solve the mystery of what was happening in the ongoing hacking of the DNC.

The contrast between them and the general mood at the DNC was dramatic. After everything that had taken place in that building in the last four months, the office was a beaten-down place. People were dragging through the day, wary of what was happening on the devices they used, what might be exposed by their daily communications, and anxious about what would be in the next WikiLeaks drop. Would it be something that would embarrass them? Cause them to lose their jobs? Expose them to danger from another vengeful group of lunatics? I had managed to boost some of the employees with my Wings and Wine Caucus, but the majority were still subdued. From the moment that Ryan and Rob arrived, it was as though there was a separate energy center in the building.

On that first day in the DNC they stayed until ten at night investigating the breach that had been announced the moment they arrived. Part of their job is to keep meticulous records of everything they find and how they respond to it. As Rob said, in the fog of war, information gets lost or misheard, and there can be a lot of false positives. They created a shared document to capture information in one place and an incident timeline to help them reconstruct what (if anything) happened. Every new piece of information went on that document.

They named this incident MIS:80, after The MIS Department, the contractor who had been running our computer system since Obama had taken office and 80, the network port that identified where the breach occurred. Of the two incidents that first day, one was a false alarm. An engineer on the staff had connected to the system via a suspicious login that set off a security alarm. Rob and Ryan tracked down the engineer to verify it was in fact he who had logged in, not an outsider to the system. Just as they were signing off on that incident, another alarm sounded in a different part of the system. They didn't know if the CrowdStrike software was identifying a new breach or an old one that they were rediscovering. Although Hacker House didn't identify the actor, this second breach was serious, and what it revealed about the vulnerability of the DNC system was even more concerning.

The MIS Department did a lot of business with the Democrats nationwide. These state organizations and campaigns connected through the DNC computer system. A political party wants to include as many people as it can in registering voters and signing up volunteers. We don't know who could be coming in through those other campaigns and state organizations. Someone getting in through Nebraska or New Mexico might be able to maneuver through the system to the computers of the DNC.

The most efficient way to be sure potential intruders were completely out of the environment and hadn't planted backdoors through which they could still get into our network was to take the scorched-earth approach: to fully rebuild the MIS:80 servers at the DNC and restart everything from scratch.

When I heard about the intensity of this first day, I was surprised by how upbeat Ryan and Rob were on the next morning's call. What they were describing was a hot mess and an embarrassment, and to me it was frustrating. By the time they arrived we had spent nearly $2 million remediating the hack, and there were still significant problems. Heather was not nearly as alarmed as I was. She said on one of the calls that what Rob and Ryan encountered was something they had all seen before. CrowdStrike had done a good job and the DNC has responded well, but working under intense pressure something always would be overlooked. Both our volunteer hackers were undaunted; in fact, they were excited. Ryan told me not to feel discouraged.

"We are firefighters," he said. "Your team here performs certain functions, but they are not an in-house security team. They manage the smoke detectors but they can't tell the kids to stop playing with matches. We face big fires."

Ryan, at 6'3" with a big red beard, almost looked like the classic Irish firefighter but Rob was slight of frame, with blue eyes, fair skin, and a runner's leanness. They both wore a uniform, though: the jeans, t-shirt and hoodie outfit of Silicon Valley.

After that rocky introduction to the DNC computer system, Rob and Ryan went with Andrew Brown to have a late dinner at Ted's Bulletin, an old-time DC joint that has great milkshakes and house-made Pop-Tarts. While they ate, they made a few big decisions about what was up ahead for Hacker House. This, they told Andrew, was not the assignment that they had been led to believe it was. They would not be mere advisors assisting the existing crew in how to improve an upgraded system. If the first day was any indication, they would be responding to live intrusions on a regular basis. The hours would be long but the work would be exciting. When you are really good at your cybersecurity job, you build such strong defenses that you rarely face a live intrusion. In this hodgepodge of a network, they would be facing them several times a week. Plus, they believed this work was vital to the election, much more important than what they had imagined when they signed up.

The team also needed more people. Rob and Ryan roughed out a list of people they were going to approach about coming to DC for a few weeks. They needed a great infrastructure person to help them gather the information necessary to make sense of the activity in more than thirty cloud accounts, several data centers and hundreds of desktops and laptops across the DNC. Each piece of the network produces data for every action taken and those actions are recorded in logs. To make this environment easier to analyze they wanted Tom Cook, an infrastructure expert who has worked at the biggest Internet service companies in Silicon Valley, to set up the telemetry.

Rob and Ryan also needed hunters: engineers who are gifted at poring through the information generated by the network logs, server monitors, applications and cloud event logs to find patterns that identify where the bad stuff is hiding. They called Chris Long and another hunter I'll call Ron because he doesn't want his name used.

Then Ryan ordered $200 worth of Soylent, a meal-replacement fluid designed in Silicon Valley that supposedly fulfills all your body's nutritional needs. Ryan believed the schedule would be that they'd get up around eight, grab some Soylent, and Uber over to the DNC for a day that would last until nine or ten at night, sometimes longer. Ryan decided he needed to buy the Soylent bars, too, as they didn't know if they'd be able to leave the computer room when an incident was underway. And Rob called his girlfriend to cancel the trip to Paris they had planned for later that month. "We can go to Paris, or we can save the election," he told her. Lucky for him, she reluctantly agreed they could go another time.

I felt like the Hacker House never turned their lights off. I was always one of the last people to leave at night, and I always saw the glow of lights in the room called "the Thunderdome." I worried that we were exploiting them. They were putting in impossible hours. I felt bad, but they said my concern was misplaced. *That's the kind of job we love*, they told me. *To find all the things that are going on that are horrible, while remaining as optimistic as possible.*

I could not believe how lucky we were to have these patriots volunteering their services to rescue us in the crucial last weeks before the election. I suppose politics has one similarity to the spirit of these cyberwarriors. Our job is to face the things that are horrible and provide hope. Yet we had come to a feeling of hopelessness and constant struggle against an elusive foe. I was not talking about the GOP candidate. I meant the Russians. After a week of these twice-daily phone calls, I felt confident that this part of our crisis was in the hands of experts.

Even the Hacker House team sensed the low mood of the DNC and wanted to do what they could to boost it. They wanted the staff to feel safer in their daily lives. The Hackers decided to become a more visible part of the DNC team. After one of the staff dropped by the computer room to tell Andrew that someone was trying to extort him through his computer, Rob worked with his girlfriend, a graphic designer, and his friend Samantha Davison, a security outreach expert, to develop a flyer. It encouraged the staff to take precautions and to come to them if anything in their computer life went awry. They placed this flyer over every toilet and urinal in the DNC. You couldn't miss it.

I thought I was as aware as the average person about how to keep my devices safe. I had learned a tremendous amount about security since my world had been torn apart by the hacking. These recommendations taught me even more:

STAY UP TO DATE—Malware depends on you working on outdated apps and devices, so staying current helps you prevent being a victim of the hacking.

2-STEP-FACTOR AUTHENTICATION—Make sure that every time you sign on to any of your networks or social media you verify that through a text message or email message to your cell phone.

SECURE YOUR PHONE—install LOOKOUT, an app
that scans your devices for malware regularly.

SHARE THROUGH THE CLOUD—Email is not safe
and thumb drives are easily corrupted. Cloud services
have security teams that work round the clock to protect
your data and are the best way to keep it safe.

Even if a flyer might sound silly to you, this was a huge boost
to the staff. People suddenly had a plan, and with a plan they felt
like they could do something to handle their anxiety about the
hacking. Staff started to stop by the Thunderdome for advice
and the Hacker House crew became a source of optimism for
all of us.

After they cordoned off The MIS Department system from
ours, the team's next effort was what they called tabletop exercises. Since the Hacker House team knew they were going home at
the end of the month, they needed to teach the in-house technology staff how to analyze the telemetry so that they could respond
to an attack. With the new visibility created by Tom's logs, the
team staged tabletop exercises, like cyber–fire drills. Hacker
House would devise an intrusion and announce it at the tabletop exercise so they could observe how the staff responded to the
event.

The first tabletop exercise, during the second week they were
in DC, was a disaster. The staff even had trouble signing on to
the system because of the new ways it had been configured by
Hacker House. The steps the staff needed to take to investigate
the breach of the system were not intuitive to our IT staff. The
team had to coach them almost every step of the way, asking
them leading questions and giving them broad hints.

There was also an emotional issue underneath the incompetence, Heather recognized. There was some mistrust among the staff. People had made mistakes. They felt bad about those and about themselves, but they also had been traumatized by the results of those errors, as had the people they worked with. Heather sensed that the tech staff was holding back, not being as forthcoming as they might be, because they didn't want to be blamed further for the situation we were in. It took many tabletop exercises and several weeks before that feeling melted away.

As the Hacker House team grew from two to five, when they discovered other problems that they needed to handle quickly, they reached out to top specialists in other areas. Some specialists they recruited were former DNC staffers who knew how to rebuild parts of the system while it was still running. Rob boasted that the team had a 100 percent recruitment rate. These top security engineers are much in demand, the hardest to hire in the industry, and usually stay at a firm for only two years before they get bored and want another challenge. Every single person they asked immediately said yes, dropped what they were doing, and flew to DC. By the end of the month sixteen engineers helped the Hacker House effort, some staying for a few nights or a full week, some sleeping on the floor of the old row house we rented for them in Northwest DC, while the core group of five remained virtually the entire time.

The Hacker House developed its own culture. They all suffered together when the Soylent bars were recalled by the manufacturer. Rob and Ryan were working so hard that they didn't hear about the recall, and the bars made them sick. Evenings when they got off before ten they sometimes went to Ted's Bulletin, because they liked the old DC atmosphere and the milkshakes and Pop-Tarts. Maybe a little too much. One night when they were home at the row house, they tried to order from Ted's Bulletin, but the restaurant was out of their favorite flavors and kept calling back to cancel different parts of the order. They reached out to other places to get their milkshake-and-Pop-Tart fix. By the end of the night, amid all the confusion, they ended up with $100 worth of milkshakes and Pop-Tarts from two different places.

Each night when they got back to Hacker House, besides the video games they played, the crew would often open up their laptops on the dining room table and share with each other the techniques and skills they had learned over the years. "It was an egalitarian atmosphere of people operating at the highest level," said Chris Long, who joined the house in mid-October. "I learned more in ten days there than I did in two years at work."

Right after ace hunters Chris and Ron arrived, we had our second big incident. On October 20, Falcon picked up an intruder using credentials that were only entrusted to system administrators and the team feared that this intruder, whom they named Airwolf, the name of the system that had been compromised, was attempting to exfiltrate data from the cloud. They spent a full week tracing back how those credentials had gotten into the hands of someone outside the system.

During this time, even Heather got a little spooked by the work they were doing. The problem of credentials was supposed to be fixed before the team arrived, but it hadn't been. One of the HH team compared it to not changing the locks on the front door after the house has been robbed. The team began to fear that there were many backdoors into the system and that they could not trust any of the remediation that had been done by the DNC.

Heather said she never thinks about who the adversary is. She likes to focus on the intellectual stimulation of picking the

problem apart, as did the rest of the team. To them it did not matter if the intruders were Russian or someone else, and besides,
figuring out who was the intruder was not their specialty. They
believed the FBI experts, but never verified whether the hackers
were Russians or not. During the Airwolf crisis, she joined our
now daily call while she was in London. It was ten in the evening there, and she had dodged outside to a chilly alleyway to
get some privacy. It suddenly hit her, as she stood in this public
place with people passing by on the street around her, that she
was discussing the fate of the U.S. election. Heather recognized
she had to be very careful about making sure our conversations
were encrypted. "It was the first time in the work I've done that
I felt personally unsafe," she later told me.

And then on October 21, they discovered Raider.

Chris discovered malware on Raider, the most important server
in the whole system. Raider was the server that all the other servers backed up their data through. Any malicious entity that
gained access to Raider essentially had the keys to our whole digital kingdom. When Chris discovered malware still running on
it, the team was shocked. They thought Raider had been taken
off the network when the DNC remediated the hacking, but there
it was still trying to make connections to servers in a foreign
country.

With the discovery of malware on Raider, the team realized
the scope of this attack might be much larger than predicted,
placing the core of the DNC's systems at risk. Heather flew to DC
and worked alongside the Hacker House crew for the first time.

One of the things that hackers needed to do was a foren-
sic investigation. Each piece of the network produces data for
every action that it takes, and those actions remain on logs that
are kept within the system. Those who specialize in forensics

know how to analyze these logs for suspicious patterns, like a piece of software that sends out a signal every five minutes or every half hour. Legitimate pieces of software might do this, too, but the malware does so to connect with a server owned by the intruder. In order to see these things, the computer logs have to be sorted and characterized so that the analyst can recognize the signal from the noise. Chris said when he looked at the possibility of sorting out this data from Raider's disc, he thought it would probably take him two or three days. Heather offered to do it for him. She was so skilled at this task she pulled it off in a few hours.

After analyzing the telemetry they understood that, if what they feared was true, they needed to act defensively. The intruders had been sitting in our voter data files for months. They had downloaded a lot of information, but they also could have manipulated what was there. Two weeks from the election, Heather and Ryan came into Tom McMahon's office to request permission to take the whole system off-line so that they could do the forensics necessary to determine if the hackers had exploited the vulnerability in Raider to manipulate the DNC's voter data. Tom was alarmed, fearing that in these crucial last days before the election the DNC system was giving campaigns false data.

"What does this malware do? Are we campaigning in the wrong places? Sending flyers to the wrong houses? Are we calling the wrong people on the phone? Are we sending Hillary to the wrong states? How do you know what this malware is doing?" he asked.

Heather and Ryan said they could not be sure, which was why they wanted to take the system off-line for four or five days to investigate. Tom agonized about this. All of the Democratic Party used these files. Were we to take the system off-line for any period of time this would cripple our election operations nationwide.

Soon thereafter the whole country would know about the problems inside the DNC.

Tom talked it over with Heather and Ryan and as he did he started to calm down. If they had been calling the wrong houses, the party would know that right away. He decided that we could not take the system off-line and would have to work with the situation as it stood.

As the team examined Raider further they discovered something frustrating about this malware. When you download a piece of software onto your computer system it resides on the hard drive. When you run the software, it makes an exact copy on the computer's memory. What Chris discovered was that the original version of the software was nowhere to be found on the hard drive. The malware that they discovered existed only in the memory of the computer. Because it no longer existed in the file system, extracting it would be extremely difficult.

Well, so what? I thought. Just get the damn thing out of there and quick. Not so fast, the Hacker House team said. Raider was so old that the existing tools to extract it from memory were not guaranteed to work. And, if we did not do this carefully, there was a good chance that extracting it would crash the system and erase the memory, including the only remaining copy of the malware. If that happened the Hacker House team would not be able to pull this piece of malware out to analyze what damage it had caused. Nor would they be able to send it to the FBI, as they did with all malware they discovered, to aid in the bureau's investigation of the hacking. Plus, they had to work quietly, because if the intruder detected that Hacker House knew about this piece of malware, they were likely to shut it down and switch to using other tactics and techniques that would be harder to detect. What they had to do was the cyberequivalent of brain surgery on an awake patient.

This was an enormous problem that needed a swift response, but it had to be done with great care. All the Hackers reached out to their colleagues in the cyberworld to get advice. The CrowdStrike team came to Thunderdome so that they all could work together to game out a response. After careful planning and consultation, plus several simulations, the extraction took only a few seconds. It worked.

At the same time that the team was wrestling with the Raider problem, they continued to train the staff through tabletops. As the staffers' skills improved, so did their confidence and their team spirit. Hacker House had to get more sophisticated in the challenges they created for the staff.

During those late nights at Hacker House, the team planted benign malware in the system for the staff to find during the table-top exercises. At one point, CrowdStrike found the malware that Hacker House planted for the staff to discover and called them on it, as if this was a prank. Crowdstrike wanted Hacker House to stop these stunts because they were stressing out Crowdstrike employees during a critical period. They compromised when Hacker House agreed to warn Crowdsrike before they planted malware so that Falcon would not be caught off guard.

As October came to a close, the staff needed less and less guidance from the Hacker team. The mood at Thunderdome was upbeat and so were our daily calls to review their progress, sometimes with Derek Parham, the deputy CTO of Hillary's campaign, also joining the call. The staff had learned so many advanced skills from Hacker House and were incredibly grateful to them. Hacker House was proud of the distance the team had traveled in such a short time, as well as being grateful to the IT staff for their energy and support. And when Raider was finally out of the system, the team seemed practiced enough to respond to incidents on their own. The hackers knew at last they could go home, telling the staff at Thunderdome to remember that they were only a phone call away.

We had a celebratory dinner on October 26 at Del Frisco, a DC steak house, the night before the Hacker House team departed, and drank a lot of very fine Japanese whiskey. I could not adequately express our gratitude to our rescuers. It had felt as though we had no one to help us until Hacker House showed up. They were one of the most remarkable things to happen in my life in politics, and until now they have received no public credit for their work.

The DNC vs. the Russians was never a fair fight, but these people made us come out the victors. This was not the kind of triumph where you see the perpetrators yanked away in handcuffs, and we knew that they would be back again. They left us with the tools and the methodology to face the next intrusion and with a big jolt of confidence that we stood a fighting chance.

There was no way to pay the Hacker House team for what they had done, but I would never forget their service.

EIGHTEEN

Comey's 18-Wheeler

Early on Sunday morning two weeks before the election, the technician I hired to sweep the DNC offices for listening devices arrived with his equipment. We'd had the place swept in September, but a lot had happened since then: the rise in personal attacks on me, the fact that Hacker House and CrowdStrike had discovered an uptick in outsiders trying to scam the staff's email addresses, and the mole sent to harass us by James O'Keefe. Of all the things I was worried about at that time, the security of the staff was never very far from my mind.

Every day I thought about Seth Rich. I had his picture on the wall of my office, along with our poster offering money to anyone who would help us find his killers. People in the office mentioned him to me frequently, some because they still missed him terribly and others because his death had made them feel unsafe. In the precious few days before the election, I did not want to increase the staff's anxiety about their personal safety. This was why I had the technician come very early on a Sunday, before anyone would be at their desks. He could get in and out before anyone besides me and a handful of the senior staff knew what he was up to.

An odd incident had occurred the week before the security sweep. The senior staff and I were meeting in Debbie's office when a woman I'd never seen before walked onto the patio area adjacent to the windows and started watering the plants, and then moved from there to start watering the orchids in Debbie's office. I did not know whether we had a contract with a gardening service, so I asked the staff. No one else knew, either. I asked Charles and his staff to search the records for one. They tried for days, but they never found one.

I didn't wait for that answer. I started moving those plants away from the chair's office. I put some in the reception area, and some more near the water fountain. I was concerned about bugs, and not the kind where you need pesticides. That was when I decided to have the place swept again.

The technician had been trained by the Department of Defense, NSA, and the Secret Service to perform this job. I only gave him a two-hour window, and he said he hoped that would be enough. It was important to me that he take extra time in the executive offices, particularly around Debbie's office and mine. He moved swiftly through the building with his ultrasensitive microphones, scanning for any anomalies in the radio frequencies. His scan was routine, uncovering nothing, until he got to the patio outside Debbie's office and mine, the place where the interns took their breaks and ate their lunches.

There he found a very strong signal, new and powerful enough to be detected in adjacent offices. The frequency was one typically used in personal locator beacons, but it was similar to the frequency technicians had found in the U.S. embassy in Moscow half a century ago that had led them to find a microphone. This frequency had not been detected when he'd scanned the same space a few months earlier.

Still the technician's report dismissed the possibility that we were being bugged. The Russians had used this technology way back in the 1950s. Wouldn't they be using something more modern and sophisticated now? I shared this information with the small group of people who knew I'd had the place swept, and the looks on their faces made the information about a Russian signal hard to dismiss. I made a point after that of watering the plants during the Wings and Wine Caucuses, and saying hello and good-bye to our Russian friends as I did. *"Do svidaniya,* Vladimir. Until we meet again."

I was trying to make light of it, but inside I was not feeling light. Not at all. I was still very concerned that we were not doing everything we could to ensure Hillary would win. No one wanted to conjecture about what would happen if she did not win. That was unthinkable.

These responses to my pleas almost made me doubt my ever-trusty gut. Everyone around me seemed so confident that this election was in the bag for Hillary. Maybe it was that people simply could not imagine that the country would elect Donald Trump to serve as president. All the terrible things he had done in the election were amplified by the terrible things he had done in the way he lived his life. Just in the last few months of the campaign, journalists had published stories about how he had cheated the contractors that had installed the glass and drapes and carpets in his casinos and other work in his hotels nationwide. He had two thousand lawsuits filed against him for not paying his workers. There was Trump University, another scam, where he charged desperate people thousands of dollars in tuition with the promise that his "faculty of hand-selected experts" would teach them his secrets about how to get rich. He never taught a single class, and the Trump University faculty was even less distinguished than he was. He had to settle that class action suit with the State of New York for $25 million just to make it go away.

And there was the problem with women. I mean, if Barack Obama had five children by three different wives, the press would have lost its collective mind about the dysfunction of African American family life. Not this guy, nor his pussy-grabbing tape, nor the modeling service he owned that relied on undocumented workers from Eastern Europe, while he was railing against illegal immigrants coming to America.

After the *Access Hollywood* tape was released, the *New York Times* published a story where a dozen women described different times that he grabbed them, kissed them against their will, or rubbed his body up against theirs as he pinned them to the wall. The stories were horrifying and, of course, he tweeted his clumsy denials. He tweeted: *"The phony story in the failing @ nytimes is a TOTAL FABRICATION. Written by same people as last discredited story on women. WATCH!"* And a few days later, the same theme: *"Nothing ever happened with any of these women. Totally made up nonsense to steal the election. Nobody has more respect for women than me!"* The one that worried me was, *"Polls close, but can you believe I lost large numbers of women voters based on made up events THAT NEVER HAPPENED. Media rigging election!"*

I had grown to think that if he was complaining about something, the opposite of what he said was happening. If he was slamming Hillary for being unethical, it was because he had so many ethical violations he lashed out at her to sow confusion. I certainly saw that in action at the second debate, when he brought up Bill's wronged women as a cover for his own bad acts. When he tweeted that he was losing the women's vote, I had a sinking feeling that his internal polls showed he was winning it.

In those closing days, I was doing all I could. With the money from Brooklyn plus our own fund-raising, I hired minority media consultants to place advertisements in black, Latino, and Asian-

Pacific Islander newspapers and syndicated radio programs, and I was very proud of that considering the resistance I faced. My concern remained the same: that we were not doing enough in communities of color. I was pulling in favors from everyone. The White House was great. I asked Joe Biden, Barack, and Michelle to record robocalls for me, and they said yes to every one. I tapped celebrity connections, getting Jeffrey Wright and Magic Johnson to write letters or make robocalls. And of course I was trying to spread around what little money I had on hand.

I was worried that we were taking too much for granted in those battleground states. The polls showed Hillary leading by double digits in Pennsylvania in the beginning of October, but by the middle of the month she was down to a seven-point lead. Inside the campaign the explanation for the drop was that old cliché that the "race was tightening." But seven points is still a huge lead. By the end of the month she was leading in Michigan by 7, Pennsylvania by 5, and Virginia and Wisconsin by 6 each, and newspapers and poll tracking firms were giving her an 80 percent chance of beating Donald Trump. Everyone was feeling fat and happy (except me) until October 28.

I was in Salt Lake City on Thursday, October 27, where I had gone to meet up with one of Brandon's FORWARD TOGETHER buses, although Brandon was manning the one on the East Coast. Utah was on our list of expansion states, and while most polls had that state as solidly Republican, some saw that support softening. We were making a play for it. This heavily Mormon state was not the kind of place willing to give the Pussy Grabber a pass. There was a chance, and a good one, that I was wrong about the electorate and that Hillary's overwhelming momentum would sweep Utah into the Democratic fold. If that was the case, I wanted to see it for myself. I would be happy to have my gloomy feeling proven wrong.

I don't remember much from that Utah trip. What I remember vividly is being in the airplane on the way back to DC that Friday—just ten days from the election—and watching Wolf Blitzer describe the letter that FBI Director James Comey had sent to the Republican chairs of the various intelligence committees in the House and the Senate stating that FBI investigators now were looking into new Hillary emails that they had just found while investigating another matter.

When I saw that, I felt like the world had just dropped out of the sky. I started emailing everyone I could think of to figure out what the hell was going on, but most people were in shock themselves. By the time I landed, the story had moved forward to not just anyone having these emails, but Anthony Weiner! Huma Abedin, Hillary's top aide, was married to that foul man. He remained under investigation for the lewd selfies he had sent, sometimes to underage girls; in one selfie, his little boy was visible in the background. The FBI had been looking through his laptop and saw a number of Hillary's State Department emails on it. Huma sometimes had used the family laptop to print out emails for Secretary Clinton, who preferred to read hard copies.

O Lord, please save us from technology, I thought. Almost every problem that came Hillary's way this election was the result of emails. They might seem as though they were making everyone's lives easier, but the way we handled them, and the way they could be falsified and manipulated, took up a tremendous amount of time and caused so much pain for her and for all of those who supported her.

I went straight from the airport to the DNC, and it was like entering a four-car funeral. When the press called, we didn't know what to say. Soon Brooklyn let us know that we should say nothing. We didn't know anything about Huma and the content of her emails, so there was nothing to discuss.

My message to the staff was that we had one more week to go, and that was plenty of time to recover from this. When you are in charge you never express remorse, doubt, or confusion. You keep the staff focused on the task and hold out hope, even if you do not feel much yourself at that moment.

I kept it together at the office but when I got home, Jeremy Peters from the *New York Times* reached me on my landline. In my emotional state, I was unguarded. He quoted me in his piece saying, "This is like an 18-wheeler smacking into us, and it just becomes a huge distraction at the worst possible time. We don't want it to knock us off our game. But on the second-to-last weekend of the race, we find ourselves having to tell voters, 'Keep your focus; keep your eyes on the prize.'"

My statement was not much appreciated in Brooklyn, where the message they had crafted was one of confidence. Comey could look all he wanted, but he was not going to find anything. I believed that to be true. I knew Hillary was an honest person, and if she had made a slip in her emails, it was not from a desire to hide anything. We had to be bold and confident. There was no other way to win this election.

In the final week before the election, I reached out to my Spook. I wanted to know his insight into what Comey was thinking by releasing this statement. My Spook was confused, too. It's a very easy thing, cyber-wise, to run a program that compares emails in one folder with another and identify the ones that are not duplicates. This was something his staff could have done in a matter of minutes to resolve the matter without announcing it to the world. Yet he chose to cast doubt on Hillary. My Spook did not see Comey as having acted malevolently, however. He reminded me that Comey had the reputation of being a Boy Scout, the kind of guy who always strived to do the right thing. The Spook did not believe that someone like Comey would deliberately tamper with the election to favor one side.

You could see the delight in the faces of Trump's campaign staff. They believed that they had the election won, and not because they had been so clever at campaigning or had such a great candidate. Comey was winning it for them. Trump was campaigning hard in Pennsylvania, Colorado, Arizona, Florida, and Michigan. His tweets were about those visits, but also about "crooked Hillary." "#CrookedHillary is unfit to serve." And: "@PaulaReidCBS: @CBSNews confirms FBI found emails on #AnthonyWeiner computer, related to Hillary Clinton server, that are 'new.'"

I had to believe the attitude I portrayed to the staff. We had one more week to go. I took out my apology list and started making calls. We need you. We need your money to help Hillary get over this. I made call after call. I asked them not to give up or give in. These were her stalwart supporters, the ones that stuck by her even though their lives had been torn apart by the hacking.

I was able to raise some money from these calls but the online fund-raising softened dramatically. As the week became the weekend, I knew there was a lot of early voting taking place, and I wanted to keep my foot on the pedal. By the weekend there was so much gossip in the media and many people were turning against Comey, but the people I worried about most were women.

In the work I was doing to get out the vote and build enthusiasm, the one thing I did not worry about was women. I figured that was Hillary's responsibility. Once Comey started to question her emails again, I feared that we were losing those college-educated white women who had been Hillary's strong supporters in the election of 2008. Were they feeling shaky about her? Had Trump's relentless campaign to discredit her made them harbor a little kernel of doubt about her ethics? If they did, something like this might turn them in Trump's direction.

By Saturday night, I felt a little bit of a backlash building. Comey had announced that he saw no problem with these newly revealed emails after the Bureau had reviewed them. Suddenly people were pissed at Comey for setting the campaign on fire. Perhaps this was going to excite the base even more. If she was down and out, she showed no sign of it in public. And her daily distributed talking points that had seemed like dry toast now had a little bit of Tabasco on them.

I had declined offers to go on the Sunday shows to talk about this, because I could not be an actress at this point in the campaign. I was just too damned scared.

On November 1, I was at the DNC when I got a call from Michael Sussmann. Earlier that day Patrice had been trying to find me and couldn't, so she'd called Sussmann to ask if I was there with him. This made him think we needed an emergency plan if something happened to me. He asked if I had a designee. I'd never thought of this before, but I instantly chose Tom McMahon, the man who knew everything that I knew about what was going on.

Later that day Rand Beers, a member of our cybersecurity task force, asked if we had an alternative place for the DNC to set up shop if something happened to the building on Election Day. Suddenly I was being asked questions I'd never even considered before—questions no American presidential campaign had been forced to consider going into the weekend before Election Day. Although I had a sinking feeling in my gut, in truth and despite the polls, I did not know what would happen.

All I knew was that I would be on a train to New York at noon Monday and see what fate awaited the nation.

NINETEEN

Election Night

On the Thursday before the election I got a call from Charlie Baker as I was arriving at a political breakfast with corporate executives featuring GOP conservative radio talk show host Hugh Hewitt and me. Brooklyn had decided to give me $1.5 million to run my Get Out the Vote (GOTV) operations in communities of color. I felt like jumping for joy! I was not going to have to spend the next ninety-eight hours worrying about raising money for yard signs, or vans to bring volunteers to barbershops where they would persuade people to get to the polls. At this stage of the campaign I knew exactly how to spend that money to be the most effective for Hillary and some down-ballot races. I knew places where there was a good candidate for sheriff who needed a bit of a boost, and some state legislators we wanted to support because they had especially promising futures. Before the breakfast, I got on the phone to spread the joy, calling organizers and officials in battleground states all around the country promising that the money was coming within the day, and we would strategize later about how to spend it.

I was worried about Virginia, even with the former governor and U.S. Senator as our vice presidential nominee. I had been in

Northern Virginia, a territory easily won by the Democrats in the last few elections. There didn't seem to be much going on there. With a little extra juice, Hillary's chances would be stronger. I also wanted to spread a little love to Ed Rendell, the former governor of Pennsylvania, because I had a gut feeling that his state could swing either way, despite what the polls and the campaign were saying. G.K. Butterfield, the head of the Congressional Black Caucus, and a representative from Durham, also had called worried about turnout in North Carolina after Hurricane Matthew. The people I was calling were those I knew from four decades of running campaigns, the ones who understood the ground game that wins an election. I was feeling less nervous about Tuesday after I made those calls.

When I got out of the event, I had a message from Brooklyn. My $1.5 milllion was now $750,000. It had been only ninety minutes from the initial call to the follow-up, and my money was cut in half.

You know I went straight to Brandon. I wanted to burn his ass at the stake for undercutting me so many times. He told me Brooklyn had decided to hold some of the money back because they were going to buy time on cable shows over the weekend. I said, "Brandon, you know colored people are not sitting at home on a Saturday night, not the ones that get out to vote. They're at a party or they're at the club. I'm only asking you to give me back the money raised by the DNC. How can you give it to me and then take it away?"

I never did get that money back. He won that one. I was angry at everyone all over again. I had already promised these states the resources. Donnie had promised Michigan $350,000 and Ed Rendell $150,000 from several unions and a big donor who wanted to help with voter protection. I wanted to target Detroit, because I feared that there was no enthusiasm there.

These old black voters like literature, particularly cards that feature Obama. There is never enough love for Obama in the African American community. When you go into a convenience store or a barbershop or a beauty salon, the images on the wall are of Jesus, JFK, Dr. King, and Barack and Michelle. I had made up cards of a photo I took of Obama hugging Hillary when she got nominated. Having Obama embrace Hillary was a message people in these places needed to see.

We needed to get those cards out, and I was still trying to get more money for North Carolina. I left the CEO event knowing that I had to go back to the DNC and start hustling up some money.

When I got back to the DNC, I went to the office and opened my blinds and looked out over the railroad tracks at the stand of trees across the way. *Hey, Vladimir! Yoo-hoo! You want a piece of me? Take your best shot. I'm done. Do svidaniya, motherfucker.* Then I threw my tired black ass into my chair, shaking my head at what a mess I had become. I had stopped cussing and screaming a decade ago, but no sooner had I gotten back in the DNC building when everything I gave up for Lent I started doing again: drinking scotch and cussing, calling people out. I could not wait for this thing to be over.

We worked the weekend, late into the night, and I managed to raise $150,000. I also arranged for some people to donate directly to state parties so they did not have to go through the DNC. We worked hard and finished well that last Sunday night at the office, the last Wings and Wine Caucus before we went to New York.

On Monday we took the noon train from Union Station. Julie, Patrice, and Julie Goodridge, who was down from Massachusetts for Election Night, grabbed seats in a back row, and I gave Tom and Charles some money to bring us back wine and beer. We were joking and drinking. For the first time in months, we felt free. What we had endured in the last two months at the DNC was going to be over soon, right after Hillary won. I knew Donnie and Tom would go back to their other jobs, and I would go back to whatever was left of my life.

While we were on the train we didn't have to think of what awaited us on the other side of Tuesday. We could rock in the rhythm of the speeding train, drink, and laugh, as we reminisced and recited from memory all the different polls and pundits who put Hillary solidly ahead. The talking points we were receiving from Brooklyn were filled with happy news. They said Hillary had ended the campaign in a very strong position, up between four and five points over Trump nationwide with early voting turnout higher than the previous elections. Early voting was up 35 percent in Florida, half of all registered voters had already exercised their franchise in North Carolina and Colorado. Also, the talking points said, it had never been easier to vote, with more polling places in many states and longer hours. As I was reading the official statement from Brooklyn on my phone I was wondering if they were talking about the same election I was.

Expressing any doubt about her victory would not be polite, or even warranted. We had given our all to this election that had troubled and terrified us in a way no election ever had before. God willing, the next evening we would be celebrating with the whole world at the Javits Center. I needed to adopt the enthusiasm of my companions on the train ride. We were going to make history!

We were like children on vacation when we all piled into our SUV and started bumping around Manhattan. We went to the hotel and scattered for the night. I ended up having dinner with my old friends Phil Donahue and Marlo Thomas at their apartment on the Upper East Side, but I didn't make a late night of it.

The campaign had two Election Day operations: the war room and the boiler room. The war room was where Robby and his political team, the communications team and the campaign lawyers, would be. Any issues with the voting machines would go there, as well as Election Day interviews for the news stations. The boiler room was not a place for press. It was in a midtown Manhattan office building on West Forty-Fifth Street. I was part of the GOTV operation and decided I needed to be there at five the next morning to begin my calls to black radio stations in the East.

I had my script down, slightly different for every congressional district. "Hillary will be a fantastic president, like the president said, more experienced on the first day than either Barack or Bill." . . . "And this is about Obama and his legacy and the way he has made us proud." . . . "Trayvon Martin, if he had lived, he would be voting for the candidate his mom is endorsing: Hillary."

As I was making these calls, I was also fielding calls about trouble in the swing states. As the polls opened that morning, problems came in from all over the country. One organizer called from Florida saying that the polls had been closed for the last hour. If some people do not vote early, they do not vote. They only give themselves thirty minutes to fulfill this civic duty, and when that thirty minutes is up, they are not likely to come back. I got on the phone with the county supervisor to find out what they were doing about this.

I was told that if I found a legal issue at a polling station, I should send it over to the lawyers at the war room. If it was a political issue, I would try to handle it. What if it was a cyberissue? We hadn't addressed that problem in our preparations for Election Day. And when these problems started piling up on top of each other, the Russians were all I could think about. We had been warned about this, but no one heeded the warning. It was as if tampering with the election on such a scale strained our imaginations, and now the unimaginable looked like it was happening on Election Day. I changed my radio script. "Now I know many of you are at precincts where the machines aren't working, or there's some trouble with your registration. Stay in line. Don't give up. Hillary needs you. Barack needs you, and so does your country. Everyone needs to vote."

In Philadelphia the polls were not open when people showed up to vote. In Durham, North Carolina, the machines had broken down. It was almost 9:30 a.m., and they still were not back up. People couldn't vote before work! I heard about a handful of problems coming out of Florida, but most of the problems were coming from Pennsylvania and North Carolina. I thought about the meeting with DHS. What if the machines had been tampered with?

In the middle of all this, the fire alarm went off, and we all had to vacate the building. I'd gotten there so early, I didn't have a security pass to reenter the building. I had to talk my way in. Fortunately I found a security guard who recognized me.

When I got back into the boiler room, it was as if I was seeing it for the first time. I had been at my desk, which was quite a mess, and completely focused on my work as the other offices and conference areas filled up that morning. This cut me off from what the rest of the people there were doing. I had a piece of paper with names of people from the DNC who had done a good job whom I wanted to suggest for positions on the inaugural committee as well as in the new administration. I walked into a meeting room where Charlie and Minyon and their team were working and handed them this paper. They took it without looking at it and set it aside.

I stood there watching for a minute, then walked down to the conference room. There was not much activity in this room. Everyone was in a good mood, certain that we were only hours away from victory. The feeling of the room was surreal to me. They were discussing which jobs they wanted in the new administration and what roles they hoped to take in the inaugural committee. Meanwhile I was starting to panic. We might lose this thing.

I went back to my desk and began my calls again, my radio spots. When Julie Goodridge came later to bring me lunch, I had a hard time taking a break. I was on the edge of bursting into tears. I felt like I was stranding people who were waiting in line. Maybe these people just needed a little encouragement to hold that place until they could vote, and if I went to eat my sandwich they would abandon that spot. This was a race that would be won one vote at a time, and we could not afford to lose even one. *Get a grip, Donna*, I told myself. *You are not single-handedly responsible for Hillary's victory.* I could only do what I could do, and I needed to eat lunch if I was going to make it through this day.

It occurred to me that maybe I was wrong. My gut might be leading me in the wrong direction. I had been so wrapped up in this cyber stuff, the idea that this election was being stolen from us by these dirty tricksters, that I had become nutty on this subject. After all, the opponent was Donald Trump. He had done so many outrageous things, too many to even count, that the end effect of all of that vulgarity and hostility had to tilt the scale toward Hillary. All the polls showed her winning, and some showed her doing it in a landslide, turning red states blue. If there were polls that showed her losing this, I hadn't seen them. My heart and my mind wanted to be in sync with the feeling of triumph, but my troublesome gut was telling me something different. Why were there so few people coming out in Detroit? All the Rust Belt cities were reporting anemic turnout in the black communities. I needed to do what I could to turn that around.

Around 6 p.m. I started getting calls from Patrice and Julie, who were nudging me to leave the desk and get to the Javits Center. I didn't think being there was the best use of my time. It was still early in the West, and there were many people to call. Plus the troubles in North Carolina and now Florida were not going away. After a while the calls and texts from my DNC staff started to infuriate me. Didn't they know that what I was doing was the most important thing I could do? Finally, I walked back to the Loews Hotel to change my clothes for an interview scheduled with Katie Couric at nine. Julie brought the car around to the lobby to fetch me.

I was surprised to find that the staff that came to New York were in the car, too. I guess they were going to strong-arm me if I refused to leave. They were in a much different mood than I was. I was the bummer in the back seat. My mood brought everyone down. I was not joking. I was very focused and had a lot on my mind.

The Javits Center seemed eerie to me. People were partying when I felt like they should be working. I saw Stevie Wonder, a man I have known since I first started working in politics, and the first thing I wanted to say was, *Can you make phone calls? We need to get people out to the polls in Detroit.* Of course that was ridiculous. The polls were closing in waves as the sun moved west across the country. I was saying the right things but not believing them. *Oh, Northern Virginia always comes in late*, I'd say, *so don't count that state out yet.* Or I was talking about our sophisticated operation that was going to bring in Pennsylvania and Michigan when the cities started to report their numbers. I know how to sound reassuring.

By the time I got done with the Yahoo interview, my heart was dragging on the floor, but I seemed to be the only one in that mood. The numbers that the Hillary campaign was releasing were phenomenally positive: Michigan and Pennsylvania Clinton +5, Wisconsin Clinton +6. Where were they getting these numbers? I had people on the ground in Pennsylvania and Florida who were reporting that there was not much activity there. I knew that it was too late to influence Michigan, and my feeling was that without a strong response in the black community in Detroit, we had lost that state. The notion that Donald Trump had cracked the "blue wall" of reliably Democratic states seemed incomprehensible to me.

People started pulling at me to take selfies with them, but it was making me crazy to be there. We still had to fight. I walked out of the Javits Center into the crowded streets of Manhattan feeling very lonely. Didn't people know? Didn't they see? I got back to my desk at the boiler room and started another round of calls.

I stayed in the boiler room until 2 a.m., even though when they called Pennsylvania for Trump I knew it was over. Michigan crushed me. I kept thinking about Donnie telling me he needed more money there and about the people I had talked to that day on the radio who needed more time to vote. I knew it was truly over when I rang up the war room and asked if we were going to keep North Carolina. They said they had called it for Trump an hour ago.

I walked into the room where Charlie and Minyon had been sitting and she told me that Obama was getting on the phone with Hillary to tell her that she had to concede. I felt so sad for her, even at that distance, and because of the distance that had grown between us during this campaign. Minyon told me that

at 1:30 a.m. John Podesta was going to address the crowd at the
Javits Center and tell them to go home. A shiver came over me,
a memory of the Gore defeat, where we had Bill Daley go out
and address the crowd because Gore was still wrestling with the
results, as I knew Hillary was tonight. With that eerie echo of
2000, I accepted that Donald Trump would be our next president. Not only that, the Russians had won.

I walked back to my hotel, head down, not wanting to talk
to anyone. The boiler room was near Trump's celebration at the
New York Hilton. His elated supporters jammed the streets.
Some of them asked me to take a selfie with them as I passed by,
but I just couldn't do it. I could not paste that smile on my face
one more time. Not tonight.

I got into my room and lay on my bed with my clothes on.
The whole thing made me numb. It was not like any other defeat
I've experienced. Sometimes you know the loss is coming, and
you can prepare for it. With Gore there was a similar feeling
of confusion and fear because the system had broken down. In
Gore we knew we would fight, and I got ready for the battle. I
was unable to sleep on that Election Night because we were up
discussing tactics. This loss was so much more devastating.

It was as if we had been battling blind. No one wanted to
believe us that the hacking of the DNC was just the prelude.
The press had misread every signal. In the final days of the campaign, when Trump said at every rally that the election was
rigged, the commentators scoffed and called him a sore loser.
He's just preparing his supporters for his humiliating loss, they
said. I remembered all the fuss about how Trump was ambigu-
ous about whether he would accept the results of the election.
If he refused to accept the results, the pundits would say, would
this tarnish the beginning of Hillary's presidency? WAKE UP!
I had wanted to scream. He's telling us flat out that it's being
rigged in his favor. But the Democrats weren't supposed to say

anything. If we started talking crazy like that, we might screw up Hillary's victory party.

As the sun came up I knew I had to leave right away. I was supposed to take the noon train back to DC with the others from the DNC, but I needed to get back. The rest of the staff would be grieving, and I wanted to be there for them. I texted Patrice as I got onto the 9:00 Acela to DC. My body felt heavy and my spirit was dragging as I slumped into my seat feeling the defeat. As the train pulled out of New York City my phone rang. It was Robby Mook.

"Madam Chair, I'm so sorry," he said. I could hear the tears in his voice. "I'm so sorry."

"I know, Robby," I said. "You did your best. You worked hard. We all did."

After we hung up, I turned off my phone. People would be calling me now as it was getting close to nine and I didn't want to talk about it anymore. We needed time to grieve. I had to muster courage to face the staff.

What would I say to them?

TWENTY

Grief and Regret

Mr. Singh was waiting to take me directly to the DNC when I exited the train from New York at noon. The weather in DC was damp, not drizzly or stormy, but more of that drip, drip, drip—like tears coming out of the sky—that had dogged the Democrats for the whole campaign. Washington, DC, felt like a tragedy had just befallen the town. I put out a formal statement from the party congratulating Donald Trump on his victory, but it felt phony to do that. This was a tradition in politics, and I wanted to make sure that I fulfilled my duty even though during the election Trump had done his best to trample all the norms and standards at every turn.

The mood at the office was heavyhearted. I could see that from the looks on the faces of Miss Natalie and Miss Barbara as they greeted me when I arrived at the office. They were trying to smile but were not really able to do so. No one had expected this defeat. Even though I had suspected it, and communicated my doubts about everyone else's certainty, I was shocked, too, and sick to my stomach, although I would not share that with the staff. I had not wanted to be right, and accepting the reality of the fact that the country had just elected Donald Trump. I started to question what more we all could have done.

I gathered as many of the staff as I could for my lukewarm pep talk. We were going to pick ourselves up and rebuild, I said, even though the week before I had discussed in detail with them how we would redeploy the staff to work on the inaugural and had asked them to make a list of those who wanted to be considered for jobs in the new administration. This was a pep talk without much pep, another tradition in our politics that seemed deadly dutiful.

I left the office early to go to Georgetown to teach my afternoon class.

I always plan my lectures weeks in advance, but this afternoon I knew I would be doing my students a disservice if I kept to that plan. I sat in my office looking at exit polls and vote totals in counties in Michigan, Ohio, Pennsylvania, and Wisconsin, states I was shocked that we had lost. I was trying to figure out how to explain this to my students and to myself.

We had lost three key battleground states by fewer than 80,000 votes. The hardest part when you lose an election, like when Al Gore lost in 2000 by 537 votes, you think that's just a few more door knocks, that's eight phone calls, it's one more rally. We had congressional seats where our candidate won, but Hillary lost the district. I wanted to do a postmortem to find out how we fell short in Wisconsin and in Michigan, and to take a look at how we got over the finish line in Minnesota, but not by much. The first thing I looked at was black women. In 2008 and 2012 black women were the highest performing voters for us in the whole country, but in this election our numbers fell from 70 percent to 64. That to me summed up how we had failed to persuade and to communicate because of our internal squabbles. To me campaigning is about persuading, but this campaign was about models and data. I knew data was important. I had used it in the campaigns I led, but my focus on energy, enthusiasm, and emotion had made me feel like a dinosaur. What electrified young people for Bernie was not data. It was the old-fashioned kind of politics that I knew, and that the party needed to know again.

Each week as the election heated up, I had given the twenty-five students in my class a lesson in real time about the future of women in politics. When the class assembled, I tossed all of the polling away. I wanted to know what the students thought. Since the pundits clearly had not known anything, perhaps these young people would be better at deciphering the loss than those of us who were paid big bucks to do this.

I never sat when I taught the class, pacing back and forth as I fielded their questions. This day I was so tired that I could not pace. I had not slept that night and emotionally I was spent. I propped myself against the desk in front of the class.

"What do you think? What happened? Where did she go wrong?" I asked them.

We went around the class and each student had a say. Many of them were so outraged that Trump had won. They kept saying that Hillary was the most qualified person ever to seek the presidency. You can count on one hand the number of women who sought the presidency: Victoria Woodhull in 1872, before the women had the right to vote; Shirley Chisholm in 1972; Geraldine Ferraro, who was placed on the ticket in 1984 when we had this rebellion inside the Democratic Party; and Elizabeth Dole, who emerged as a very qualified woman on the Republican side in 2000. Hillary really was the most well positioned to run for the presidency, in terms of name recognition, party support, and resources.

My notes from that day are about our choice between a change candidate, whom a majority of Americans found odious and repugnant, and the Democratic nominee who had been on the national stage for more than twenty-five years. The vast majority of Americans disliked both candidates. But the preliminary exit polls had Clinton winning by thirteen points on who was best qualified. Her net favorability was five points higher than Trump, 36 to 41. In terms of the right temperament, she won by twenty points, 49 percent to 29 percent. And on honesty, she won 34 to 31 percent. Still, voters didn't know her and trust her enough to put her in the White House.

I learned two things from the students. One was that they disliked identity politics. They thought that Hillary spent too much time trying to appeal to people based on their race, or their gender, or their sexual orientation, and not enough time appealing to people based on what really worried them—issues like income inequality and climate change. The other takeaway was the misogyny of the media, something we had talked about every week in class. And we talked about the Electoral College. And then I finally said to the students, 2016 will be remembered for how the playbook changed on how to run for President.

My class ran from 3:30 to 6:00 p.m., but at 5:15 I dismissed class early. This was the only time in my life that I thought I would fall asleep at the wheel driving home. I went to get Chip at Betsy and Mia's, and to say hello to Kai. When Chip and I got home, the feel of the house was eerie. There were no more hang-up phone calls on my landline, and no death threats or racial or sexist insults shouted into my voice mail. Just a message from Martin O'Malley and one from David Simas, Obama's political director, checking in. Chip knows my routine is to sit in front of the television and watch Rachel Maddow, and he has his place on the sofa where he watches, too, but I didn't have any more tolerance for politics that night. Bernie called to see how I was doing, and to ask me if I intended to stay on as chair. I certainly did not.

I had a speech to give in Florida that week. I'd agreed to speak, thinking I'd be in a good mood to address a crowd about how Hillary won, but I had to change to looking toward 2018 and 2020. My heart wasn't in it at all. When I arrived in Florida I got a call from Suze Orman inviting me to come join her and her wife, Kathy Travis, for dinner at their home and not talk about the election. My CNN buddy Ana Navarro was right when she told me after a defeat like this you find out who your friends are. Suze and KT invited me to stay the weekend, but I really wanted to be home.

In the months after the election, closing things out at the DNC was a full-time job that demanded all my energy. Besides my work to arrange the Future Forums, I wanted to make sure steps were made to build the DNC infrastructure back up. To do that I had to have some tough negotiations with Brooklyn about the ownership and use of the DNC voter data. I hired my best friend, Betsy Marvin, to represent me personally in my capacity as the interim chair because I had become uncomfortable with some of the agreements that were consummated before I took on that role. Namely, the agreement that gave the Clinton campaign control over the party's finances before Clinton was the party's nominee. To me this seemed shady enough that it might produce a lawsuit and I wanted to be fully protected. Ultimately, the negotiations were amicable, albeit time consuming, but the end result gave me peace of mind that the DNC was well positioned to grow into the organization it once was.

I finally was able to address my problems with Brandon, but it was a soft kind of firing. Like other staffers, he was laid off as it was the end of the campaign. I did not want his family to have a rough landing, and I also wanted to make sure they had health insurance, so I kept him on staff for one more month.

The world I had around me had something of a surreal quality to it. Many of the things that I had learned in the FBI briefing in August about the Russian interference in the election were now becoming headlines. On December 16, at his last press conference, President Obama said about the Russian hacking of the election that he had told Putin to stop it, and that Putin had stopped. I knew Putin and the Russian intelligence services had not stopped until Hacker House gave us a way to fight back.

On January 6 President Obama ordered the director of national intelligence to declassify a report about Russian interference with the election. The report said our intelligence agencies were certain that Putin had mounted a campaign to influence the election and had chosen as his clear favorite Donald Trump. The report detailed the hacking of the DNC, the trolls, and the well-timed and carefully chosen leaking of the DNC emails, which were intended to disrupt Hillary's progress. It even talked about hacking the voting machines in several states, but would not say that this affected the outcome of the election.

I didn't have that feeling of relief that overtook me in October when the Department of Homeland Security said essentially the same thing. I knew saying this would have no impact, as it hadn't then. Sure enough, Donald Trump and his crowd did not take this as a warning that something should be done to secure our electoral system. He railed against the report's conclusions, saying it was just a partisan attempt on the part of the outgoing administration to delegitimize his victory. He even accused Obama of tapping his phone to distract from the content of the report. When he did things like that to me it was a sign that he knew, better than the intelligence agencies were willing to admit, how much the Russians had helped open the door for him to enter the Oval Office.

Later in November Seth Rich's parents, Mary and Joel, came to town so that we could fulfill a promise we made to each other when I visited them in Nebraska in October. We had pledged then that we would not allow Seth's death to become another DC police cold case.

We met with Mayor Muriel Bowser and that weekend we put up flyers on light poles all around Bloomingdale/LeDroit Park offering a $20,000 reward to anyone who came forward with information. The day was cold and blustery, but we were determined to remind people of the beautiful soul Seth had been. Some Trump supporters were promoting the baseless conspiracy theory that Seth had been murdered by the DNC because he was the one who had leaked our emails to WikiLeaks.

One of Trump's supporters hired a private detective who was describing this theory on Fox News, and it was getting some airplay. Each time it died down they found some reason to pump it up again, despite the fact that there was no evidence to support it. At first I couldn't believe that these people were so cruel that they would not leave these grieving parents to heal. Then I did believe it, because of what I knew of the character of my former opponents. The thing I could not believe was that we were going to have to endure four years of this.

As the Rich family and I made our way around the neighborhood, my heart filled up with some hope that our country would survive this. Despite the cold weather, people on the street who saw what we were doing wanted to help. When the tape we were using proved to be too weak to get the flyers to stick to the light poles in the wind, people went home and brought us duct tape. They took handfuls of flyers to put up in their grocery stores and cafés. When we finished our work that day I was reminded of the fundamental decency of most Americans, how they want the best for each other and that most of us are more human than we are Republican or Democrat. That was the country I wanted back.

A month after I stepped down as chair of the Democratic Party, I went to Nebraska to attend a fund-raiser for a summer camp Seth had attended when he was a young boy and where his parents were setting up a memorial fund. At home I sat Chip down, and we had a talk about the newly quiet life we were going to lead. I told him Momma was putting away her two-day suitcase and her one-week suitcase. She wasn't traveling anymore. She was going to set things right here at home.

I was not reading about politics in the two newspapers I got every morning. I was looking in the style section and on the sports pages for the first time since I was a child. February had been unusually mild, giving me hope that soon I'd be able to work in my garden again, but March turned up chilly and snowy, creating a yearning in me to get my hands back in the earth. I knew that once I had my garden going again, I would have a sense of rebirth.

There was one matter I had to settle that month to clear the way for a peaceful and productive spring. I had to make my amends for the scandal that erupted over the leaked email showing I gave the death penalty question to Hillary before her March 2016 town hall with Bernie.

I wrote an op-ed for *Time* magazine that reviewed the many bad actions the Russians had taken to skew the election in Trump's direction. I also wrote about how the leaks had thrown our campaign strategy off course and explained how we never got it back. I described the way WikiLeaks chose the emails to do the maximum damage at precise moments in the campaign and how the trouble those caused sidelined key actors like John Podesta and me. My intent was to write a call to action that we never let this happen again, but also I wanted to take responsibility for the damage that leaked email with the question had caused the Hillary campaign. Even if I couldn't remember sending it—and couldn't find it in my online files—there was no proof that I had not sent it. The best course was for me to apologize, and I did:

> Sending those emails was a mistake I will forever regret. By stealing all the DNC's emails and then selectively releasing those few, the Russians made it look like I was in the tank for Secretary Clinton. Despite the strong public support I received from top Sanders campaign aides in the wake of those leaks, the media narrative played out just as the Russians had hoped, leaving Sanders supporters understandably angry and sowing division in our ranks. In reality, not only was I not playing favorites, the more competitive and heated the primary got, the harder DNC staff worked to be scrupulously fair and beyond reproach. In all the months the Russians monitored the DNC's email, they found just a handful of inappropriate emails, with no sign of anyone taking action to disadvantage the Sanders campaign.

The press reported the apology as an admission of guilt, and I knew that was what they would do. I just wanted this episode to be over. After a few moments in the news cycle it was. I took another whipping, with the hope that this would be sufficient, but the issue follows me still and seems to be one that will forever.

You know, fuck 'em. I have a playful side, but I also have Delores, the part of me that is spitting mad and not afraid to fight. If people look at all I have done in my life and define me by that one questionable incident, they are no friends of mine. At this point in my journey on this earth I no longer care what they think of me.

I had to take time to heal from the PTSD of that crazy campaign. Kai was still crawling, but he was trying to get up on his feet to walk. I told Betsy and Mia that they could count on me for babysitting any time. I bought a crib for Kai and put it in the room next to my bedroom. I even had Chip on alert. Kai was a bit too rough with the dog, so Chip knew when it was his cue to find a place to take a nap. When I looked out at my garden, I started planning what I would plant with Kai and Chip in mind.

In April, when it was only a few days before I could start to dig in the dirt of the garden, I took Chip for his annual wellness exam. They wanted to give him his rabies and distemper shot. I resisted because the dog was thirteen years old, and I thought he didn't need that kind of thing again. They insisted, but Chip balked. He's not a whiner, but he did whimper when the needle went in.

That afternoon when I came home from the grocery, Chip met me at the back door and led me over to his bed where there was blood on his mattress. I asked Libby, Betsy and Mia's dog who often stayed at my house, if she had bitten Chip, but she just looked confused. She's not a biter. Chip gave me a look of sadness. I called the vet and told her Chip was bleeding and she said to bring him right in.

After taking a look at him she asked, "Did he eat poison?"

I said, "No. Chip wouldn't even eat steak unless I put it on a plate."

She drew his blood but then she noticed that the problem was that it was not clotting.

"Why?" I wanted to know.

"I don't know, but he might have had poison," she said.

"No, Libby's the one who goes hunting, but Chip never goes hunting. Chip eats off his plate. And the plate has to be above the floor."

"Well, we're going to have to draw more blood from the jugular vein," she said.

He didn't cry. He was always stoic. As I was bringing him home, he threw up blood and then he excreted blood. I called Betsy.

"He was fine this morning when I got Libby," I said. "He wanted to play ball."

She rushed home from work and when she saw him she said, "I think Chip is dying."

We took him over to Friendship Animal Hospital, where they gave him a blood transfusion and drugs to get his blood to clot. His blood platelet count went from 47 when he arrived to 22. I feared he would have a stroke. We decided about six in the morning that we did not want Chip to suffer. His last act was to kiss Betsy on the nose, where he would always kiss her, as if to wipe away her tears. We took turns holding him until he passed, and it was the lowest moment that I'd felt in a long, long time.

That April I did plant my garden, and it is beautiful now as I write this in the summer of 2017, but the house is not the same and neither am I. I said to myself that I would never let politics break my heart again, and there it went ahead and did, and worse this time than any of the others. Donnie Fowler Jr. has been counseling me that I need to get back out in the mix. "You have to bring us to that mountaintop like you always do, Donna," he said to me last time we spoke. He wanted me to speak of the goodness I see in people's striving to make their lives better and the hope that grows inside them and me and the communities all around this land.

For now, though, I have to consider what politics can be for me and for us as a country going toward 2018. My heart was not the only one that was broken by the election of 2016, and if we are going to heal this partisan divide we need to find a way different from any we have devised before.

Choose Hope, Choose Action

April was my month to break down because I didn't know how to get up, and I had no urgency to do so. I lost my dog, I lost my voice, and then it felt as if I had lost everything. After fourteen consecutive years of teaching, I took a leave from Georgetown in the spring semester. I gave up my consulting clients when I took on the job as interim chair, so I had no work to go back to, but it wasn't like I was sleeping in. I had lost my place in the world, my sense of my country, and it seemed as though the things I valued were not what my fellow citizens valued anymore.

Before I took the job at the DNC, I was giving speeches and making appearances at forums and events several times a week. I had a checklist for every day of my life. I had a weekly column to write, or a television appearance, or a class to teach, or I was helping candidates raise money. After Election Day my phone didn't ring much at all. In the silence, I started to doubt myself. Had I been too cocky taking on the job of running the DNC?

I thought that, with my instincts to guide me, this job was not going to be hard, but it was harder than anything I'd ever faced. Maybe those boys in Brooklyn had been right about me. I did not want to show anyone how frightened I had become and how weary I felt from the constant bombardment of people wishing me nothing but bad luck. And I was disheartened worrying that this was a feeling that would never go away.

As April turned into May, I came to appreciate how I was not alone in feeling like this. In a way I want to thank Donald Trump for bringing me so low, because in that state of mind I was connected to my fellow Americans. Before the 2016 campaign, I had been doing well for a good long while, and then— poof!—it was over, and there was reason to think that it might not start up again. I know many of Trump's supporters felt the same about their lives.

This election burned it all down—broke all the rules and destroyed the traditions of civility—but after a firestorm passes what comes up first is hearty and strong. As a country we are back down to the fundamental questions: Who are we? What do we value? Can we find a way to trust again and not just see each other as partisan enemies? Can we remember that we have more in common as Americans than the issues that divide us?

Most Americans work hard every day to try to make a life out of the things that matter. They get up, get their kids off to school, get to work, come home, and try to live within their means. Everyone dreams of a better life for themselves and for their children, while at the same time so many of us feel as forgotten, as my sister and her neighbors did begging for some Hillary yard signs. We have been trained not to ask anybody for anything and to be a little ashamed when we have a need that we cannot meet on our own. We have pride and we cherish our independence.

Donald Trump is an extraordinary salesman. He knew how to exploit those grievances by deepening them instead of finding a way to address them. He put his supporters in this huge box, cut them off from the rest of the country, and said, "We are going to make America great again because everyone else but you has abandoned those American values. They have put other people's interests before your interest, and I'm going to take care of you. I alone can fix it."

As I write this, we're well into President Trump's first year in office, and he has not been able to fix anything. He and his supporters are getting a lesson in real time about how in this country no person alone has the power to "fix it." In America we don't let others fix things for us. The best solutions, the best connections to each other, come from working together. It's never been clearer that all voices need to be heard as we look toward the future.

After I was taken down by the election, I knew I had to go back to the basic values that drew me into politics. From the very beginning I have been interested in protecting and expanding the right to vote. In this election our democracy was weakened by multiple forces. Republicans, Democrats, and independents became convinced that the election was rigged. Elections have been rigged right from the beginning against people who did not own property, slaves, women, minorities of all kinds, and sometimes against a party by gerrymandering. Never had I seen a candidate who promoted this in his stump speech, but then again no one had ever seen anyone like Donald Trump.

While Trump refuses to admit that the Russians hacked our election, I lived it. I saw how it impacted the lives of everyone around me. The Russians may have not changed the totals in the voting machines, but they confused us, inflamed our doubts and our worst impulses, and destabilized the Democratic Party, making it an unfair fight. They paralyzed a significant portion of the electorate with all these disruptions. We're a country of more than 320 million people. In 2016, 69 million voted for Hillary, 66 million voted for Donald Trump, and 90 million eligible citizens did not vote.

To this day it is astonishing to me that we do not treat this as a national emergency. Fair elections are the foundation of our collaboration, our unity, and this is something we all agree on. The heads of the intelligence agencies and members of Congress predict our 2018 election hack is coming, but there have been no moves to block this next assault on our democracy. Both parties should come together to take the necessary steps to protect the ballot box in 2018 and beyond, but the chaos sown by the hacking still reverberates in our politics and in our media, preventing us from feeling hope and taking action.

As I sat in my rocking chair on the porch in the last few months trying to come to terms with what happened in the wretched election of 2016, I found hope by remembering Hacker House. Those engineers represented the best of America. To them it was not important who won. All they cared about was having a fair fight. They gave up their comfortable lives, their friends and families, to live in a run-down row house to put their values into action. They could have stayed home, but they chose to act. That simple patriotism and love of the truth and fairness got lost in the turmoil and abuse of 2016, but I know it is within us, and I want to focus my future on bringing that spirit back.

When you've gone through such a soul shaking, the way out of despair is faith. Despite the deflection, dishonesty, and distraction we all lived through in 2016, I still have faith in the American people. I believe that, like the team from Hacker House, we all want a fair fight. The only way we can restore vigor to this process is to widen the franchise, get more people involved, and make them feel the power of participation. For this I thank Donald Trump once again, as opposition to him and his policies has increased citizen participation to levels I have not seen in decades. More people are insisting that their voices be heard, and it is our patriotic duty to hear each other out.

It was late in April, just before college graduation season, when I realized that 2017 would be the first time in more than a decade that no institution had asked me to give a commencement address. At the end of April I got a call from Miles College, a historically black college in Alabama. I was excited to say yes, because I knew that so much had happened in the last year that this speech would not be like any of the other fifteen I'd given.

I tried to put some thoughts on paper, but they just would not come to me. I wanted to give the students hope, even if I was having a hard time feeling it myself. Who wants to be the person with a pessimistic message on one of the happiest days of these people's lives? When you have nothing, you go to prayer. I was praying on it, praying on it all the way to the airport. Then the flight was delayed. Another huge storm.

I was in the airport asking, "Oh Lord, let this be the last storm." Within an hour and a half, the storm had pulled out farther into the Atlantic, and we were on the last flight to Birmingham.

On the flight there, I did not write. I was frightened by the storm that was not too far to the east. The clouds were roiling, black as night, and the lightning was amazing, but we had the smoothest flight I'd ever had through a storm. I started to write about the storms that had followed me all through the election, and how I took them as signs at each stage about the darkness that enveloped our country for those months. All the while I was writing I was envisioning Chip on my lap looking out the window helping me stare down the storm. As we circled to land, I jotted down on my notepad: "Choose Hope, Choose Action."

I got to the hotel close to 11 p.m., and the words started coming. I described how in the last two months I had taken an inven-
tory of my life. This was not as easy as figuring out what's in
your pantry or how many shoes you have. This was not about
material things, but about the qualities in me that I knew I could
always depend on. I told the graduates not to be complacent
or discouraged when the storm clouds came their way: Choose
Hope. Choose Action. And I ended on this quote, "You'll be
surprised to know how far you can go from the point where you
thought it was the end."

In 2005 I thought Hurricane Katrina was the end of my
hometown, New Orleans. Nearly 1,800 people died in that
storm, and thousands more lost their homes after twenty feet
of water poured over the levees and into the streets. The country watched those people at the convention center, who had lost
everything, standing there begging for someone to come to their
rescue. My huge, extended family was scattered across the country. I thought we'd never be together as a family again, because
we saw from Katrina that no one cared what happened to the
people of New Orleans.

Then the American people saw the ravages of neglect on the
faces of those people. They did not turn against us. They didn't
stick their noses up and say, *Well, you're on your own.* They wel-
comed us. They brought us in and they fed us. They put money
in our pockets. Thousands of volunteers donned Hazmat suits in
ninety-degree heat and worked stripping mold from the houses
that remained after the waters receded. And although George
W. Bush took a lot of heat for how the government responded,
he recognized his mistake and worked to correct it. As a board
member of the Louisiana Recovery Authority, I was part of one
of the most extensive rebuilding efforts in our country's history.
I was in and out of the Bush White House as much as I was when

Obama lived there, as we worked to repair homes, rebuild the levees, and bring people back to the Gulf Coast. As a country we chose hope for the Gulf region, and we put those values into action.

I choose to hope that we are learning the lessons of this election and that they will bring us together as a country. I also recognize it's hard to know what to do next. My faith has always been my strongest attribute. My grandma Frances taught me early on to rely on the power of prayer to gain strength. But, it was my dad, Lionel, who taught me to never surrender and to fight for my country—no matter what.

Katrina tested my family's values, our connection to each other, and our capacity to trust each other when the time was bleak and scary. When we came through, it strengthened those values by putting them into action. We chose hope, and I believe this is what our country will choose, too.

The outcome of the election was such a gut punch. People have rightly taken to the streets and social media to protest outrageous actions by the new administration. I worry, however, that our daily dose of outrage from the Tweeter in Chief tends to obscure larger lessons for our democracy.

I've worked for four decades in the trenches for the Democratic Party and its candidates. This election reminded me, however, that as much as I love my party, I love my country more. Free and fair elections are the bedrock of our democracy. The Russian hacking of 2016 showed us that—without intense vigilance—our electoral process is deeply vulnerable to tampering. That should terrify every American. Let's take the terror and turn it into action. We must ensure our democratic institutions are strong enough to withstand the cyberattacks of the future.

In the summer of 2017, I was named a visiting fellow at the Shorenstein Center on Media, Politics and Public Policy at

Harvard University. I pledged to use my time there to explore what can be done to shore up our defenses against a hostile foreign power trying to influence our election. My hope is that, after reading my story of the hacking of our elections, you will want to do your part, too, in reclaiming and safeguarding our democracy.

Choose hope.

Donna and Chip, 2015

Timeline of the Hacking

April 29, 2016: DNC discovers their systems had been breached and immediately contact the FBI and CrowdStrike.

May 16: DNC officials meet with senior FBI officials to discuss the hacking.

June 10–11: DNC kicks the hackers out of their systems. New hacking attempts continue on a regular basis.

June 14: *Washington Post* publishes an article publicly revealing that the DNC had been hacked by Russian intelligence.

June 15: Guccifer 2.0 starts posting documents online claiming to have hacked the DNC, Hillary Clinton, and other Democrats. The documents include a "Donald Trump Report" dated December 2015, fund-raising documents, and national security memos.

June 18: Guccifer 2.0 posts additional documents, alleging that they are financial and personal data from the DNC and its donors.

June 20–21: Guccifer 2.0 releases a document called "Dossier on Hillary Clinton from DNC."

June 28: Another site, DCLeaks, releases emails allegedly from the account of Sarah Hamilton, a Hillary for America advance staffer.

June 30: Guccifer 2.0 posts an "FAQ" that includes attacks on Hillary Clinton and praise for Donald Trump, calling his political "position straight and clear."

July 6: Guccifer 2.0 releases documents purported to be the DNC's "action plan" for the Republican National Convention and a draft release on Democratic National Convention platform committee members, among others.

July 14: Guccifer 2.0 releases additional documents alleged to be hacked from Democrats.

July 19: Donald Trump officially becomes the Republican Party's nominee for president.

July 22: WikiLeaks releases first batch of emails they claim were authored by staff at the DNC.

July 24: Debbie Wasserman Schultz resigns; Donna Brazile appointed interim chair.

July 25: DNC releases statement apologizing to Bernie Sanders, his supporters, and the Democratic Party for the "inexcusable remarks" contained in the leaked emails.

July 25–28: Democratic National Convention in Philadelphia, PA.

July 27: Trump, in a news conference, says, "Russia, if you're listening, I hope you're able to find the thirty thousand emails that are missing."

Late July/Early August: Trump campaign surrogates, RT, WikiLeaks, Roger Stone, Julian Assange, and others push the conspiracy that Seth Rich's murder was connected to the DNC hack.

August 2: DNC bolsters general election staff.

August 4: The Department of Homeland Security contacts the DNC regarding the hacks. The DNC provides information to DHS soon after.

August 8: Roger Stone claims he is in contact with Julian Assange and suggests more WikiLeaks releases are coming.

August 11: DNC memo announces a cybersecurity task force.

August 12: Guccifer 2.0 releases documents they claim to have hacked from the Democratic Congressional Campaign Committee (DCCC). WordPress subsequently removed documents due to a "valid complaint regarding the publication of private information."

August 15: Guccifer 2.0 releases documents alleged to be from the DCCC related to Florida primaries.

August 18: DNC breach notification sent to democratic donors, stakeholders, and others.

August 21: Guccifer 2.0 releases documents alleged to be from the DCCC related to Pennsylvania primaries.

August 31: Guccifer 2.0 releases documents alleged to be from the DCCC related to Nancy Pelosi.

September 13: Brazile statement on release of additional documents.

September 15: Guccifer 2.0 releases documents alleged to be from the DCCC related to New Hampshire, Ohio, Illinois, and North Carolina.

September 21: DCLeaks releases emails alleged to be from Ian Mellul, HFA advance volunteer.

September 23: Guccifer 2.0 releases documents alleged to be from the DCCC called "Dossier on Ben Ray Lujan."

September 26: First presidential debate.

September 30: DCLeaks releases emails allegedly from the account of Beanca Nicholson, HFA volunteer.

October 4: Guccifer 2.0 releases documents alleged to be from the DCCC and falsely advertises them as Clinton Foundation documents.

October 4: Vice presidential debate.

October 5: Hacker House team arrives at the DNC.

October 6: DCLeaks releases emails alleged to be from Capricia Marshall.

October 7: *Access Hollywood* Trump tape story breaks.

October 7: A joint statement from the Department of Homeland Security and Office of the Director of National Intelligence names Russia as source of DNC hack.

October 7: WikiLeaks releases first batch of Podesta emails.

October 9: Second presidential debate.

October 10: At his campaign rallies Trump promotes WikiLeaks, saying things like, "WikiLeaks, I love WikiLeaks!" and encouraging Americans to read the Podesta emails saying, "WikiLeaks has some new stuff. Some brutal stuff . . . Just trust me, it's real bad stuff."

October 14: Yahoo investigative reporter Michael Isikoff publishes a story on the fake email from John Podesta to Donna Brazile contained in the WikiLeaks dump.

October 17: DNC meets with DHS officials.

October 18: DNC Chair Brazile sends letter to RNC Chair Priebus requesting that the two major parties work together to fight the cyber warfare.

October 18: Guccifer 2.0 suggests release of additional DNC documents about Donald Trump and promises there is more to come.

October 19: Final presidential debate.

November 1: DCLeaks releases emails alleged to be from the account of Zachary Leighton, HFA advance staffer.

November 4: Guccifer 2.0 falsely claims to have registered with the FEC to be an election observer, warning Democrats may rig the election. (In fact, people cannot register with the FEC to be an election observer, and the claim looks like an attempt to depress voter turnout.)

November 6: WikiLeaks releases second batch of emails alleged to be from the DNC.

November 8: Election Day

November 9: WikiLeaks releases final batch of Podesta emails to date.

December 9: Based on a secret assessment by the agency, the CIA informs U.S. lawmakers of its conclusion that Russia conducted operations to assist Donald Trump in winning the White House.

December 29: The Obama administration announces sanctions against Russia for its interference in the U.S. election.

January 5: Director of National Intelligence James Clapper and National Security Agency Director Michael Rogers testify before the Senate Armed Services Committee. During the hearing, Clapper says the intelligence community has grown more "resolute" in its assessment that Russian intelligence was involved in the hacks aimed at the DNC and Podesta and that Russia poses "an existential threat" to the United States.

January 6: The Office of the Director of National Intelligence releases its report on Russian activities in the U.S. election.

Acknowledgments

Gratitude. I am truly grateful for all of the support that I have received in writing this book.

To Robin Sproul, a well-known, respected journalist and former Washington, DC, bureau chief and vice president of ABC News, for encouraging me to write my story and for introducing me to her son-in-law, Matt Latimer, and his partner, Keith Urbahn, at Javelin. Javelin has become one of the fastest-known and fastest-growing literary agencies in Washington, DC.

Matt and Keith inspired me to take stock of everything I experienced and write it down. They took my notes and turned it into a strong proposal. Matt and Keith became my advocates who encouraged me to not give up when I was simply too exhausted to relive the 2016 campaign.

To Robert Barnett, my longtime agent and friend. Thank you for believing in me for so many long years. Onward!

To a brilliant, first-rate, and inquisitive editor, Paul Whitlatch, along with publisher Mauro DiPreta, associate publisher Michelle Aielli, publicity director Joanna Pinsker, marketing director Michael Barrs, assistant editor Lauren Hummel, and the entire team at Hachette Books for your constant support, encouragement, edits, and team spirit. Paul even came down to Washington, DC, to keep us moving. Thank you for doing your job so well.

To Danelle Morton, my hero—or, in the words of America's poet, Maya Angelou, "a phenomenal woman"—who helped me write this book. Danelle brought her A game to the table and the typewriter. For two solid months, she pulled out her tape recorder, listened to my story, took copious notes, and interviewed dozens of my former colleagues. She did a remarkable job of fact checking, research, editing, and writing. She captured the party's inner turmoil, the hacking, the remediation process, and the day-to-day struggles of the closing weeks of the campaign. With a great sense of humor and an ability to understand the monumental threats we faced, Danelle encouraged me to tell this story and stood by me as I completely broke down and started my healing process. Without Danelle's great reporting skills, this project would have been languishing on my desk for years. She's now part of my Who Dat family.

To my former colleagues at the Democratic National Committee (DNC), who contributed to my recollection of events and the actions we undertook during the worst cyber nightmare in U.S. history. Let's start with former ASDC chair and NH party chairman Ray Buckley and DNC finance chair Henry Muñoz, who went with me to FBI headquarters for a very thorough briefing on the DNC's hacking and the Russian attempts to destabilize our democracy. Thank you, Ray and Henry. The nightmare isn't over, so let's remain vigilant.

To the other officers—R. T. Ryback, Stephanie Rawlings-Blake, Andy Tobias, Grace Meng, and Maria Elana Durazo— for supporting me in every way through the fall campaign and beyond. You're my heroes. You're in my thoughts and prayers for life.

To the DNC's council chairs, caucus chairs, standing committees, and state party leadership, and all of our volunteers, donors, and stakeholders, bless you. Bless you. Bless you. I am proud of my twenty years of service. We opened doors, expanded participation, fought to include those formerly excluded from political leadership. Yes, we nominated the first black man to win the presidency. We did make history together. It's now up to you to help get a woman into the White House. Yes we can!

To the entire staff at the DNC. I love you all. You're my family for life—thank you for your courage, tenacity, and steadfastness in the face of danger, personal insults, harassment, and much more. Some of you never knew of or understood the danger that came our way. But, you came in every day, weekends and holidays included, to work to help our first female nominee fight to become president of the United States. We came back from a massive debt to compete, and we raised funds for Democrats up and down the ballot. We all owe you a debt of gratitude for your commitment to the cause of justice and equality for all. To the Research, Tech, Digital, Comms, and political staffs, I never lost faith in any of you. Party Affairs and Finance, you're amazing, too. Alecia Dyer, let's not forget those who served. Thank you, team.

Although we came up short, I am still in awe of the workload and long hours of the entire DNC team. Your dedication to the cause made a huge difference. I look forward to returning as an intern again—but I'm done with being your leader.

To Pratt Wiley, Hannah Fried, Will Crossley, Greg Moore, Kevin Jefferson, Seth Rich, and everyone who has contributed to and believed in the DNC's Voting Rights Institute, Fannie Lou Hamer would be damn proud of all of you. The right to vote is sacred, and we must continue to fight for every eligible citizen to vote and have it counted. And let us not forget to restore the 1965 Voting Rights Act.

To the best researcher in American politics, Lauren Dillon, for your help in keeping a great timeline on the entire hacking of the DNC.

Special thanks to the following DNC staff members, consultants, and members of my Wings and Wine Caucus.

First, Donnie Fowler Jr. He's my son from another mother's womb. I fell in love with Donnie when I hired him for the Gephardt 88 campaign. He's been at my side in every major political battle, so when I became chair, I called Donnie to join me. He left behind his beautiful wife and two young daughters to spend the fall campaign in Washington, DC. His tech savvy combined with his grassroots organizing ability made him the perfect seat mate for the final weeks of campaign 2016. Donnie was my eyes and ears on the ground. Bless you, Donnie.

To Anne Friedman, my other child from another mother's womb. She not only kept up with my erratic schedule, she ensured that I had something to eat every day (so what if it was healthy) and made sure I got to my various destinations safely. Although Anne is Jewish, she served as one of my outreach captains to the Black Lives Matter movement and kept me informed of their activities. She became one of their advocates and also did major battle for the DNC's outreach to millennials.

To Mike Lux, my longtime friend and progressive warrior. Early on, Mike took my call and came over to the DNC to help build ties between the progressive community and the DNC. Mike wasn't just an advocate, he was the leader who helped me reach out and build consensus, and helped shape our closing argument on some of the media we sponsored at the DNC. Mike brought along his extensive Rolodex and was instrumental in helping the DNC raise much-needed funds for the final months of the campaign. Without him, the party could not have provided resources to state parties and down-ballot races often ignored in presidential races.

To Adam Parkhomenko, Leah Daughtry, Brian Bond, John Neffinger, Zac Petkanas, Kandie Stroud, Cynthia Jazzo Rutundo, and many others whose service went beyond the role of a party strategist or consultant. You all are damn good warriors. God is not done with you. There's one more fight in all of you.

To Julie Greene, Patrice Taylor, and Charles Olivier— founding members of the Wings and Wine Caucus. Don't worry, I will never share our secrets, late night talks over at the "Club," or hanging out in Denver, Colorado. You all kept me sane. You made me laugh, and you never wavered in your support of the DNC. You played it straight and by the rules. We pulled five major events together in less than six weeks. We knew there was no room for any errors. And we didn't flinch. You are more than my coworkers, you're members of my family. Thank you.

Special appreciation to a longtime friend, warrior, and strategist, Tom McMahon. When I saw you at the DNC Convention in Philadelphia, I said to expect my call: You responded, and I am deeply grateful for your leadership. As the anointed cochair of the Wings and Wine Caucus and my designee—just in case—I am forever mindful that some of us are called to serve. Thank you for responding to the call to service and for helping me rebuild the fifty state strategies. When I told you that I wasn't going to get paid but insisted that you get paid because you're a father of four kids, you resisted. There's no easy way to say thank you, but I hope that your children will one day know how brave and tough their father was in helping to save the party from the extreme hacking that was done. The party owes you a debt of gratitude.

Finally, to the cybersecurity task force led by Michael Sussmann at Perkins Coie, Nicole Wong, Aneesh Chopra, and Rand Beers, you all taught me more about cybersecurity, protocols, and much more. Special thanks to the brave men and women of Hacker House. You're some of the badasses in the cyberworld. And I mean that in a good way. To Shawn Henry, and Dimitri at CrowdStrike. Thanks for helping us clean up the mess created by the Russian meddling and interference. Your remediation services throughout allowed us to build stronger.

To the many staffers and volunteers working in Brooklyn at the DNC or HVF headquarters, thank you for moving away from home to help the team up at HFA. To Bernie Sanders, Martin O'Malley, and the other presidential candidates, your support enabled me to do my job as interim chair. To Julie Goodridge, whom I met on one long, hot summer day—your insights, love, and support was invaluable throughout the campaign. Good luck in all that you're doing to make this a more just world.

And to my dearest of friends, Elizabeth L. Marvin, whose wise counsel and special bond helped me figure out the impossible and stay afloat. Her legal advice, along with her colleagues at Lewis Baach Kaufmann Middlemiss PLLC, enabled me to focus on the campaign and not all the legal stuff that comes up throughout a long and entangled political season. When I needed clarity, you provided sound and wise advice. Thanks to Jeffrey Robinson, Eric Lewis, and your assistant for being part of my team.

To Mia Coffman, a proud Navy veteran, Betsy's partner, and my friend who can handle herself in an alley fight, thank you for providing me with delicious meals (shout-out to Hello Fresh), midday humor, and for reminding me to get back on my bike. Of course, you made me buy a bike, too, but riding again helped to jog my memory and get out of my house.

You also brought a special little angel into my life—Kai Wolf Coffman-Marvin. While you recuperated, I was one of his babysitters. For six weeks, I held this little boy in my arms, and he made me smile again. Now he's walking and calling me Nana. Betsy and Mia, you know what it means to be part of the Who Dat family. Thank you for allowing me to insert myself into your lives until I could get back to my own. Our weekend meals, yawl tolerance for my crazy hours, for keeping Chip beyond the call of friendship, for endless meals, support, love, prayers, watering my plants, grabbing my mail, helping me navigate a new security system and protocol, and for checking on my house and allowing me to vent in a no-judgment zone. Your friendship means the world to me.

Kai, with those bright blue eyes. I look forward to watching him grow up and, of course, teaching him how to dance.

To another son from another mother, Adam Talbot. You're talented, and I can't thank you enough for helping me during some tumultuous storms.

To David Kusnet for your keen insights and intelligence. For helping me understand the breaking news from the perspective of working people. And to David Dreyer, for keeping me grounded and focused on the day-to-day struggles within our party.

To the AFL-CIO, AFSCME, AFT, SEIU, Teamsters, Laborers, UAW, Carpenters, Machinists and other major international unions who once again pulled out the stops to help us register new voters, organize vast numbers of communities, and help us raise much needed funds for voter protection and turnout, I am proud to be not only a member of two unions, but so very grateful for your support over my long years in politics and organizing.

To my colleagues at Georgetown University, including my TA, Jeanna Galper, the Women and Gender Studies Department, and all my students. Thanks for your steadfast support.

A special thank-you to my neighbors in Crestwood, my colleagues at Brazile and Associates—my great assistant, Ro'Chelle Williams; my editor, Neil Scott; the most talented and most supportive writer, Bruce Cherry; pollsters Stefan Hankins and Cornell Belcher; my IT and tech guru, Dan Hopkins (Mr. Two Steps); and the late David Kaufmann, who taught me so much about acts of goodness and kindness. To my former editor, Clint Hooker, and colleagues at Universal U'Click. Special thanks to all my former editors and colleagues at *Ms.* magazine, *Essence* magazine, and *O, the Oprah Magazine.*

To President Barack Obama, for fulfilling one of my dreams to serve as a member of the J. William Fulbright Foreign Scholarship Board. And to Vice President Joe Biden, for those special "Black on Black" meetings.

To my former colleagues at CNN. I miss y'all, especially the hair and makeup crew and so many wonderful producers and former producers like Lucy Spiegel. You all taught me to "stay calm and carry on." And to my colleagues at ABC News, especially George Stephanopoulos, Robin Roberts, executive producer Marc Burstein, Jonathan Greenberger, Mae Joo, Kate Bosland, Kerry Smith, and so many others, including Elena George for outfitting me and encouraging me to wear those mink eyelashes. Thanks for allowing me to be part of the team that won an Emmy.

Last but never forgotten—my large and extended family. You have always been in my corner. Your love and support keeps me strong and picks me up when I stumble. Our parents raised us to stick together, and you continue to stand by me—warts and all.

My phenomenal sisters Cheryl, Lisa, Demetria, and Zeola— all I can say is you are my role models and personal heroes. I know that it's often tough to place you and your family in the line of target, especially in the heat of a presidential campaign. Rest assured, I will continue to try to live up to our mother Jean's high standards.

My amazing brothers Chet and Kevin—whose strength matches that of our late father, Lionel. Your prayers were truly amazing. I heard your prayers when you sent those words: "No weapon formed against Thee shall prosper."

To my many nieces and nephews who kept me posted on family gossip, sent me their grades (go Brianna and Chet Jr.), shared family photos, posted favorable things about their Aunt Donna when I was under attack, and came up postelection for our traditional New Orleans–style Thanksgiving meal, I love you all from the bottom of my heart.

To all my cousins and especially Louis Smalls, Tina Yancy, Gina Theis, and Michael Brown—y'all kept texting me to stay the course. Your prayers were powerful and I am grateful beyond words.

I will never forget the many friends who wrote, called, or texted me to encourage me to stand up. Your thoughts and prayers were indeed a powerful blessing to me through the many storms. Special thanks to author Iyanla Vanzant, my longtime mentor Eleanor Holmes Norton, longtime friends Dr. Toni Luck, Priscilla Perkins, and Julia Hudson, my healing sisters Sherry Dmytrewycz, Sandra Andacht, Dr. Andrea Sullivan, Dr. Sonya Chawla, and my acupuncturist Dr. Ni, the amazing financial guru Suze Orman, my New Orleans cup buddy, Mary Matalin, and lawyer, TV whiz, and friend Greta Van Susteren—sisters for life.

If I left anyone out, it wasn't because you're forgotten or unloved. I will never forget you—for you not only prayed for me, you had my back.

To Mr. Singh who never failed to be there to pick me up and was always on time. Mark Penn for encouraging me to get back on the saddle, along with Michael Eric Dyson. To Henry Louis "Skip" Gates and Glenn Hutchins, who helped me to stay calm in the storm and find my way back to shore. To Elaine Kamarck, who introduced me to the Spook. And yes, to the Spook, who kept me steady.

This book is for all of you—and for our great country. But I urge everyone to remember what former Senator Ted Kennedy taught us in defeat when he said "the work goes on, the cause endures, the hope still lives, and the dream shall never die."

I'm proud to be an American.

INDEX